# A–Z

of

# WHITEWORK

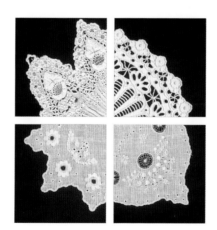

SEARCH PRESS

# Contents

"On white linen the silk of gray shadows"

Denise Levertov

First published in Great Britain 2015

Search Press Limited
Wellwood, North Farm Road,
Tunbridge Wells, Kent TN2 3DR

First published in Australia by
Country Bumpkin Publications
© Country Bumpkin Publications

ISBN: 978-1-78221-179-2

The Publishers and author can
accept no responsibility for any
consequences arising from the
information, advice or instructions
given in this publication.

**Suppliers**
If you have difficulty in obtaining
any of the materials and equipment
mentioned in this book, then please
visit the Search Press website for
details of suppliers:
www.searchpress.com

Printed in China

# Introduction

"Whitework seems to have been done all through the ages in almost every country of the world. Sometimes it was in the ascendancy of fashion, sometimes overshadowed when other types of embroidery gained more attention. But it was always there – the delicate Indian Muslins, the crisp white cuff that contrasted so beautifully with the Elizabethan's sparkling gold and silken sleeve, the Scandinavian openwork or the finely wrought Scottish baby bonnet – serving its purpose as a washable lightweight decorative cloth for shirts, underwear, bed pillows, coverlets, baby clothes, shawls, dresses, and altar linen."

*From Erica Wilson's Embroidery Book*

Whitework is a general term that covers embroidery techniques as diverse as the exquisitely fine, delicate stitches of Ayrshire work and the bold, vigorous knots of Mountmellick and candlewicking.

Despite their differences, all share the identifying characteristics of white thread stitched onto white fabric, the texture of the stitches creating wonderfully subtle patterns across the surface of the fabric.

Throughout history, whitework has been practised in some form by most civilisations and cultures, beginning with the ancient Egyptians. Such is the appeal of this type of embroidery that designs and techniques have been borrowed and adapted throughout Europe and Asia to produce distinctive embroidery styles with universal appeal.

So many styles and techniques fall under the umbrella of whitework that it is impossible to include them all here. Hence, the focus of this book is on surface stitchery and cutwork – those techniques that do not count or manipulate the threads of the ground fabric. These will be covered in a future publication.

As you turn each page of this book you will discover wonderful techniques and stitches; some will be familiar while others will lead you to new and exciting discoveries. You may choose to use them as tradition dictates or in new and innovative ways: regardless, enjoy the undeniable magic that they bring.

# Ayrshire Embroidery

Also known as Scottish sewed muslin, the Flowerin', tamboured muslin, sewed muslin.

Ayrshire is the name given to the delicate, fine, white stitchery that was produced in Scotland in the first half of the 19th century. Named after the county of Ayr in south-west Scotland, Ayrshire was worked onto translucent cambric and muslin and is now often associated with christening gowns and bonnets. So popular was this form of embroidery that it was one of the few styles of whitework to be developed into a commercial industry, flourishing between 1820 and 1860. At the height of its popularity the demand was so great that the sewing was sent out of Ayrshire to other parts of Scotland and even to Northern Ireland.

Identifying characteristics of this type of embroidery are the extensive use of satin stitch, stem, herringbone, overcasting, blanket, eyelet and chain stitches, contrasting with cut areas filled with dainty needlepoint lace fillings, all worked onto sheer muslin or cambric. The majority of designs were floral giving rise to the term 'the Flowerin' or 'the Flowering' and the title of 'Floo'erers' or 'Flowerers' that was given to the embroiderers. Although this style of embroidery is sometimes referred to as 'tamboured muslin', there is no evidence that it was worked with a tambour hook rather than a needle.

## HISTORY

Scotland has long associations with the production of fine linens and delicate embroidery, both for use in the home and as a supplement to the family income. Most women were accomplished needleworkers and when, in 1814, a sewn muslin agent, Mrs Jamieson of Ayr, introduced designs and techniques that she had copied from a French christening robe that had been brought to Scotland by Lady Mary Montgomerie to her workers, a cottage industry rapidly developed.

Designs were professionally drawn and the patterns often so intricate that they had the appearance of lace. Initially, the designs were printed onto the muslin with wood blocks and rollers rubbed with a blue bag, but as printing techniques developed, a lithographic press was used.

Once the fabric was marked, including the manufacturer's name and number of days permitted to finish the piece, it was delivered to the outworker to be stitched, then the finished embroidery was returned to Glasgow or Paisley to be made into a garment. It was the function of an agent to distribute, collect and pay the workers. Embroiderers worked at piece-work rates that were equivalent to carpenters, builders and farm workers. Only the best embroiderers were permitted to work on the most intricate pieces. Agents carried detailed samplers and purchasers would specify the quality, amount of work and type of needlepoint fillings when ordering. As in all commercial work, the purchaser paid for the quality.

By the 1820s, Glasgow had become the main centre for this industry and there were 34–40 large

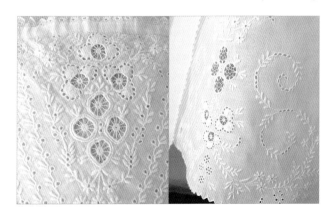

"Although the surface stitchery has great textural richness, Ayrshire is intended to be seen against the skin or shadowed undergarment, so displaying its translucent quality and the value of its filling."

*Gay Swift, The Batsford Encyclopaedia of Embroidery Techniques*

manufacturers based there. They employed more than 400,000 outworkers throughout the west of Scotland and Northern Ireland.

A considerable amount of work was carried out in factories and by 1850, thousands of women were employed in this way, labouring a seventeen hour day to earn the meagre sum of fourpence. Several women worked on one piece, depending on their area of expertise. The embroiderers who specialised in the delicate needlepoint lace fillings were paid a higher rate than others. Even small children were utilised, paid halfpence a day to thread an endless supply of needles.

Although many writers would lead us to believe that this embroidery was a joyous and enjoyable pursuit, the reality for many impoverished women was exploitation by astute organisations and endless hours of sadly repetitive and demanding work.

The fineness of the embroidery and the lack of adequate lighting meant that the workers strained their eyesight terribly and the women took to bathing their eyes in whiskey to revive them.

The majority of the finished garments were destined for export to the United States and Europe but some were for sale in Britain. Women often embroidered christening gowns and bonnets for their own, and relatives' children, copying the professional designs and making up the garments themselves. These gowns were quite distinctive in style, designed with a V-shaped panel from shoulder to waist that came to a point where it joined the skirt. Behind the lower edge of the V, an opening was left in the skirt/bodice seam.

Long gowns were worn by girls and boys but when worn, the point was tucked in for a girl and left out for a boy.

The gown skirt featured an inverted V panel with the weight of the design coming down to the hem where it was best displayed.

These magnificent gowns were handed down through many generations of families. A drawstring at the neck and waist enabled easy adjustments so that the gown could be worn by differently sized children. These gowns are often breathtaking in the beauty of the designs and fineness of stitching and Ayrshire embroidery is widely regarded as one of the most technically superior forms of needlework.

The cotton fibre that was spun and woven into fine fabric and embroidery thread was imported from the United States and the outbreak of Civil War in 1861 led to an end to this trade. This was the major cause of the decline and collapse of the Ayrshire embroidery industry. The development of machine embroidery in Switzerland enabled many of the motifs to be mass produced and made large-scale hand industries less commercially viable.

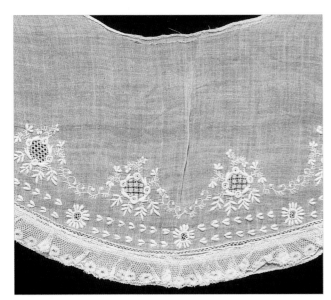

*Section of a collar, circa mid 1800s*

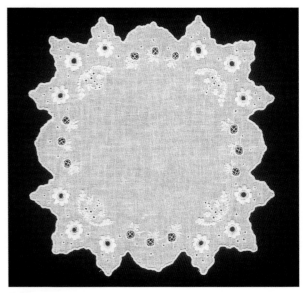

*Doiley, contemporary*

## Materials

### Fabrics

Traditionally, Ayrshire embroidery was worked onto fine, translucent cotton muslin (lawn) or linen or cotton cambric. There is no equivalent available today for cambric but good quality Swiss or Italian cotton lawn is the most suitable for mimicking traditional muslin. Fine cotton batiste can also be used but it does not have the body of lawn and it is more difficult to see the individual fabric threads.

Launder fabric before using to remove sizing and to pre-shrink. Press well and starch if the fabric is too limp.

Cambric is a finely woven linen or cotton fabric that was first made of linen in the northern French town of Cambrai. Cambric's dense weave and superior smooth hard finish made it one of the most popular and versatile fabrics for nearly four centuries.

Muslin is a general name for plain woven, fine white cottons for domestic use, including lawn. It is believed that muslins were first made at Mosul (now a city of Iraq). They were widely made in India, from where they were first imported to England in the late 17th century. Muslin was first woven in Scotland in 1780 by James Monteith of Blantyre and from then formed a large part of the Scottish weaving trade. Swiss muslin is a modern, crisp, semi-transparent fabric, either dyed or white, and sometimes figured. Certain sheetings are known as muslins. Bookbinders' muslin, made in Scotland, is fine and crisp.

### Threads

Fine white sewing cottons such as D'Alsace or Broder Machine no. 50 from DMC most closely resemble the traditional embroidery threads. Experiment with fine embroidery threads such as Anchor Coton à broder no. 40, DMC Broder Spécial no. 30, stranded cotton and linen and cotton lace making threads. The fine needlepoint lace filling stitches require a finer thread than the surface embroidery.

### Needles

Use sharp or crewel needles, sizes 10–12 being most suitable for fine fabrics and threads. Continually move the needle along the thread to prevent excessive wear in one spot. Use a fine tapestry needle to work the needlelace fillings.

### Other

An embroidery hoop was traditionally used to work only the needlepoint lace fillings and all other embroidery was worked in the hand. This enabled the outworkers to stitch much more quickly – important when time is money.

Use a hoop when you feel that you need help keeping the fabric tension correct. Bind the inner ring of the hoop with cotton tape or bias binding to protect the fabric and to help maintain a consistent tension. Check the hoop tension regularly and adjust when necessary.

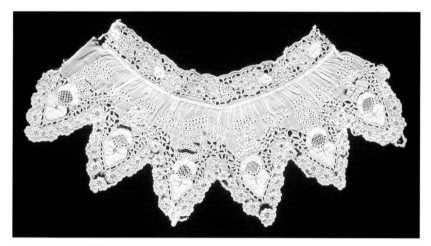

*Engageant, late 1700s*

### STITCHES FOR AYRSHIRE EMBROIDERY

| | | | |
|---|---|---|---|
| Blanket stitch | Herringbone stitch | Satin stitch | Stem stitch |
| *detached* | Laddering with | *flat* | Straight stitch |
| *edging* | overcast stitch | *slightly padded* | Trailing stitch |
| Chain stitch | Outline stitch | *highly padded* | |
| Cloth stitch | Overcast stitch | Side stitch | |
| Eyelets | Net stitch | *single, double* | |
| *pierced, flower* | *single, double* | Spanish point stitch | |
| *linked* | *buttonholed* | | |

# CHAIN STITCH

1 Secure the thread on the back of the fabric and bring it to the front at A.

2 Take the needle from A to B, using the same hole in the fabric at A. Loop the thread under the tip of the needle.

3 Pull the thread through until the loop lies snugly against the emerging thread.

4 Take the needle through the same hole in the fabric at B and emerge at C. Loop the thread under the tip of the needle.

5 Pull the thread through as before.

6 Continue working stitches in the same manner.

7 To finish, take the needle to the back just over the last loop.

8 Pull the thread through and secure on the back.

## St Gallen

Textile art has played an important part in the history of this small town in eastern Switzerland since the 13th century. In the 19th century it was an important centre for the manufacture of fine muslin and an exporter of French style hand embroidery. It also became a centre for machine embroidery and as the importance of this grew, hand embroidery became largely confined to the mountainous part of Appenzell. Here it still survives as a cottage industry today.

The St Gallen Textile Museum has an extensive collection of whitework handkerchiefs, collars and cuffs that were created between 1850 and 1900.

# CLOTH STITCH

*Lace fillings are worked within a cutout area that is edged with blanket stitch, overcast stitch or trailing.*

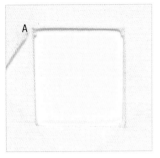

1 Secure the thread on the back of the fabric and bring it to the front at A, on the upper left hand side.

2 Take the needle to the back at B and emerge within the opening. Ensure the thread is under the tip of the needle.

3 Pull the thread through.

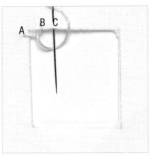

4 Take the needle to the back at C and emerge within the open space. Ensure the thread is under the tip of the needle.

5 Pull the thread through as before.

6 Continue working stitches in the same manner until reaching the right hand side of the opening.

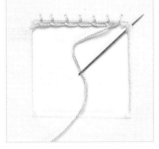

7 Take the needle from back to front through the opening on the right hand side.

8 Pull the thread through. Take the needle from back to front through the opening on the left hand side.

9 Pull the thread through to form a long straight stitch just below the row of loops.

10 Take the needle behind the first loop in the previous row and the long straight stitch. Ensure the thread is under the tip of the needle.

11 Pull the thread through.

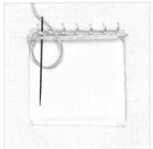

12 Take the needle behind the next loop in the previous row and the long straight stitch. Ensure the thread is under the tip of the needle.

## CLOTH STITCH *CONTINUED*

**13** Pull the thread through as before.

**14** Continue working stitches across the row in the same manner.

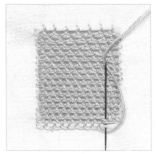

**15** Continue working back and forth across the opening until it is filled. In the last row, take the needle through the lower edge of the fabric for each stitch as well as behind the loop and straight stitch.

**16** After the last stitch, secure on the back.

# EYELET – FLOWER

**1** Work a pierced eyelet following the instructions on page 35. Do not end off the thread.

**2** Bring the thread to the front on the outer edge of the eyelet at the twelve o'clock position.

**3** Work four satin stitches to the right, beginning each stitch at the edge of the eyelet.

**4** Work a second layer of satin stitches over the first layer, using 5–6 stitches.

**5** Bring the thread to the front at the three o'clock position.

**6** Work a petal in the same manner as before.

**7** Bring the thread to the front at the six o'clock position and work a third petal.

**8** Bring the thread to the front at the nine o'clock position and work the final petal.

# LADDERING WITH OVERCAST STITCH – METHOD ONE

1 Work two parallel rows of running stitch. Keep the stitches small and close together. Work the ends in running stitch.

2 Using an awl, pierce the fabric at the left hand end between the two rows of running stitch.

3 Bring the thread to the front at A, just beyond the first running stitch beneath the hole.

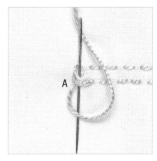

4 Take the needle through the hole and emerge just to the right of A.

5 Pull the thread through and work a second overcast stitch just to the right of the first.

6 Using the awl, pierce the fabric to make a second hole just to the right of the first.

7 Take the needle to the back just over the upper line of running stitch and between the two holes. Pull the thread through and emerge through the second hole.

8 Work overcast stitches around the thread and fabric, between the two holes, until reaching the lower edge.

9 Work two overcast stitches along the lower edge of the second hole and running stitch.

10 Using the awl, pierce the fabric to make a third hole just to the right of the second.

11 Work the bar following steps 7–9. Continue over-casting and making holes and bars to the end of the line of running stitch.

12 Overcast the right hand side of the last hole, finishing at the upper line of running stitch.

# LADDERING WITH OVERCAST STITCH – METHOD ONE *CONTINUED*

**13** Take the thread through the hole and bring it to the front, just above the upper line of running stitch and above the last hole.

**14** Work two overcast stitches into this hole.

**15** Continue working right to left across the row, working two overcast stitches into each hole.

**16** Finish by overcasting the left hand side of the first hole.

# LADDERING WITH OVERCAST STITCH – METHOD TWO

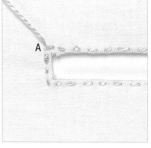

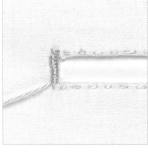

**1** Work two parallel rows of running stitch. Work the ends in running stitch. Cut inside the rectangle as shown.

**2** Fold back the fabric in line with the marked outline and finger press.

**3** Bring the thread to the front at A in the upper left hand corner.

**4** Following the instructions on page 15, overcast along the first folded edge.

**5** Work overcast stitch from left to right along the lower edge in the same manner. Stop when you reach the position for the first bar, B.

**6** Take the needle to the back on the opposite side just over the upper line of running stitch.

**7** Pull the thread through and take the needle to the back at B again.

**8** Pull the thread through and again take the needle to the back on the opposite side.

9 Pull the thread through to complete the foundation bar.

10 Following the instructions on page 70, work overcast stitch along the bar until it is completely covered.

11 Continue overcasting along the lower edge until reaching the position of the second bar.

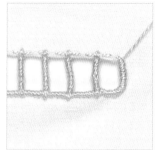

12 Work this bar in the same manner as the first. Continue until all bars are worked. Overcast to the end of the running stitch and along the right hand end.

13 Working from right to left, overcast the upper edge.

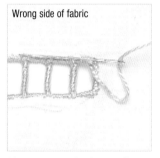

Wrong side of fabric

14 To secure, take the needle through the stitches on the back and pull through.

Wrong side of fabric

15 Using small sharp scissors, cut away any excess fabric beyond the stitching.

16 Completed laddering.

# OUTLINE STITCH

1 Draw a line on the fabric. Secure the thread on the back of the fabric and bring it to the front at A.

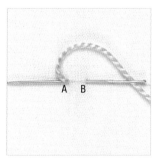

2 With the thread above the needle, take the needle to the back at B and emerge at A.

3 Pull the thread through to complete the first stitch.

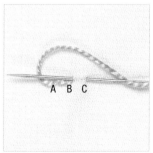

4 With the thread above the needle, take the needle to the back at C and emerge at B.

## OUTLINE STITCH *CONTINUED*

5 Pull the thread through to complete the second stitch.

6 Continue working stitches in the same manner, always keeping the thread above the needle.

7 To finish, take the needle to the back for the last stitch.

8 Pull the thread through and end off on the back.

# OVERCAST STITCH

1 Work a line of back stitch (see page 43) or running stitch (see page 40) for padding.

2 Secure a new thread on the back and bring it to the front near one end of the padding.

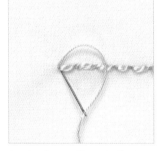

3 Take the needle to the back, directly opposite, on the other side of the padding.

4 Pull the thread through to form a stitch that is at right angles to the padding.

5 Work a second stitch in exactly the same manner, positioning it alongside the first stitch.

6 Continue working stitches in the same manner.

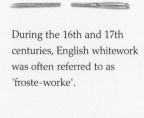

During the 16th and 17th centuries, English whitework was often referred to as 'froste-worke'.

# NET STITCH – SINGLE

1 Secure the thread on the back of the fabric and bring it to the front at A.

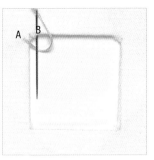

2 Take the needle to the back at B and emerge within the opening. Ensure the thread is under the tip of the needle.

3 Pull the thread through.

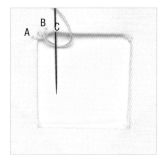

4 Take the needle to the back at C and emerge within the open space. Ensure the thread is under the tip of the needle.

5 Pull the thread through as before.

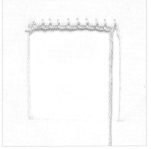

6 Continue in the same manner until reaching the right hand side of the opening.

7 Take the needle from back to front through the edge.

8 Pull the thread through. Work 2–3 overcast stitches down the right hand edge.

9 Take the needle behind the last loop in the previous row. Ensure the thread is under the tip of the needle.

10 Pull the thread through.

11 Take the needle behind the next loop in the previous row. Ensure the thread is under the tip of the needle.

12 Pull the thread through as before.

## NET STITCH – SINGLE CONTINUED

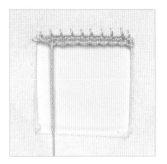

13 Continue working stitches across the row in the same manner.

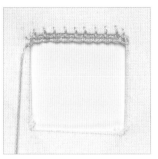

14 Take the needle from back to front through the edging on the right hand side and work 2–3 overcast stitches down the edge.

15 Continue working until the opening is filled. In the last row, take the needle behind loop and through the fabric's lower edge for each stitch.

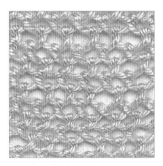

16 After the last stitch, secure on the back.

## NET STITCH – DOUBLE

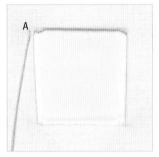

1 Secure the thread on the back of the fabric and bring it to the front at A.

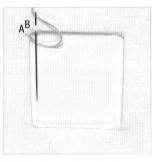

2 Take the needle to the back at B and emerge within the opening. Ensure the thread is under the tip of the needle.

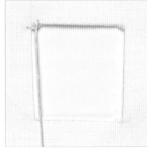

3 Pull the thread through.

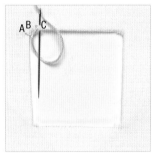

4 Take the needle to the back at C and emerge within the open space. Ensure the thread is under the tip of the needle.

5 Pull the thread through.

6 Leave a small space and work a second pair of stitches in the same manner.

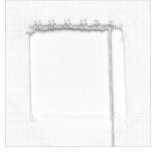

7 Continue working stitches in the same manner until reaching the right hand side of the opening.

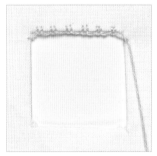

8 Work down the edge following steps 7–8 on page 16.

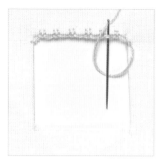

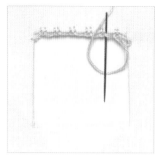

**9** Take the needle from top to bottom behind the last loop in the previous row. Ensure the thread is under the tip of the needle.

**10** Pull the thread through.

**11** Take the needle from top to bottom behind the same loop in the previous row. Ensure the thread is under the tip of the needle.

**12** Pull the thread through as before.

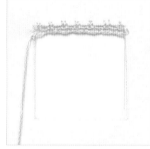

**13** Working from right to left, continue working stitches across the row in the same manner, ensuring two stitches are worked into each loop of the previous row.

**14** Take the needle from back to front through the edge on the left hand side and work 2–3 overcast stitches down the edge.

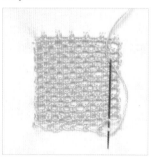

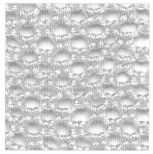

**15** Continue working rows back and forth until the open-ing is filled. In the last row, take the needle behind the loop and through the lower edge of the fabric for each stitch.

**16** After the last stitch, secure on the back.

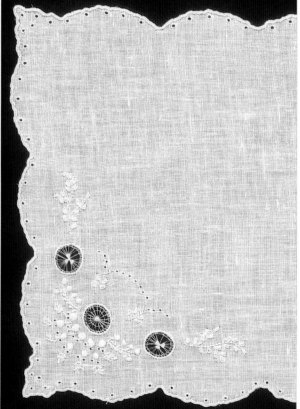

*Ayrshire embroidered handkerchief, contemporary*

# NET STITCH – BUTTONHOLED

**1** Secure the thread on the back of the fabric and bring it to the front at A.

**2** Take the needle to the back at B and emerge within the opening. Ensure the thread is under the tip of the needle.

**3** Pull the thread through.

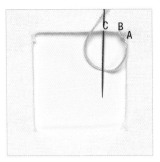

**4** Take the needle to the back at C and emerge within the open space. Ensure the thread is under the tip of the needle.

**5** Pull the thread through as before. Continue working stitches in the same manner until reaching the left hand side.

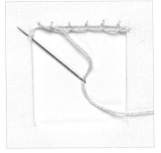

**6** Take the needle from back to front through the edge on the left hand side.

**7** Pull the thread through. Take the needle from top to bottom behind the last loop in the previous row. Ensure the thread is under the tip of the needle.

**8** Pull the thread through until it wraps firmly around the loop.

## Chikankari

*Chikankari* in Bengali means 'very nice thing'.

It epitomised refinement, taste and wealth – it was so fragile that items "survived only three washes and were then thrown away".

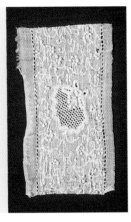

**9** Work 1–2 more stitches around the same loop in the same manner.

**10** Work approximately six stitches around the next loop of the previous row in the same manner.

# NET STITCH – BUTTONHOLED *CONTINUED*

11 Working from left to right, continue across the row in the same manner. Ensure the same number of stitches are worked into each loop.

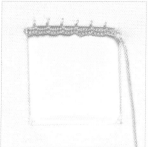

12 Take the needle from back to front through the edge on the right hand side. Work 2–3 overcast stitches down the edge.

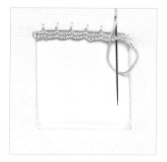

13 Take the needle behind the thread between the last two groups of stitches. Ensure the thread is under the needle tip.

14 Loosely pull the thread through.

15 Working from right to left, continue across the row in the same manner.

16 Repeat steps 6–13 to complete the second row.

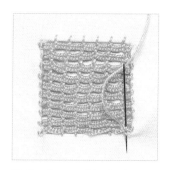

17 Continue working back and forth across the opening until it is filled. Couch the loops of the last row to the lower edge of the fabric.

18 After the last stitch, secure on the back.

# SATIN STITCH – FLAT

1 Secure the thread on the back of the fabric. Work an outline of split stitch around the shape.

2 Bring the thread to the front at A, just outside the outline.

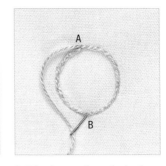

3 Take the needle to the back at B, just over the outline and directly opposite A.

4 Pull the thread through. Emerge next to A, angling the needle from under the outline.

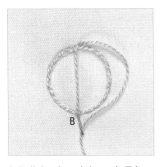

5 Pull the thread through. Take the needle to the back of the fabric next to B.

6 Pull the thread through to complete the second stitch.

7 Continue working stitches in the same manner. To finish, take the needle to the back for the last stitch.

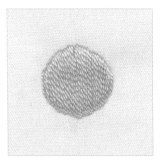

8 Pull the thread through and secure on the back.

## Dresden Embroidery

*Dresden detachable cuff, 18th century*

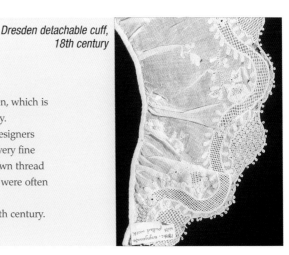

This beautiful style of embroidery is named after the German city of Dresden, which is also famous for the pillow laces it has been producing since the 16th century.

Dresden embroidery has a lacelike quality. It was made by professional designers and skilled workers for the use of the wealthy nobility and was worked on very fine cotton or silk fabric. The filling stitches utilise pulled thread, rather than drawn thread techniques, as well as coral stitch, back stitch and chain stitch. Floral motifs were often outlined with double back stitch (shadow work).

The earliest surviving examples of Dresden work date back to the late 17th century.

# SATIN STITCH – SLIGHTLY PADDED

1 Draw the shape to be filled on the front of the fabric. Secure the thread on the back. Outline the shape with split stitch.

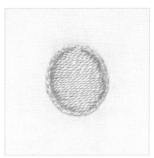

2 Bring the thread to the front just inside the outline. Work satin stitches across the shape, starting and ending each stitch just inside the outline.

3 Alternatively, work rows of chain stitch, starting and ending each row just inside the outline.

4 Secure a new thread on the back of the fabric. Bring it to the front at A, just outside the outline.

5 Take the needle to the back of the fabric on the opposite side of the shape and just outside the outline.

6 Pull the thread through and emerge on the opposite side, very close to A.

7 Pull the thread through. Continue working stitches in the same manner until the shape is completely covered.

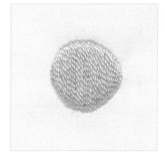

8 To finish, take the needle to the back of the fabric after the last stitch. Pull the thread through and secure on the back.

# SATIN STITCH – HIGHLY PADDED

1 Draw the shape to be filled on the front of the fabric. Secure the thread on the back. Outline the shape with split stitch.

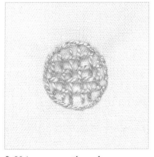

2 Using coarse thread, work rows of darning within the outline.

3 Continue adding layers of darning until the shape is the desired height.

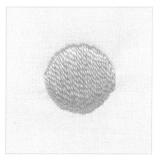

4 Cover the darning and the outline with satin stitch following steps 4–8 above.

# SIDE STITCH – SINGLE

1 Secure the thread on the back of the fabric and bring it to the front at A.

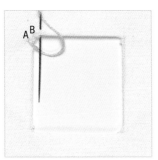

2 Take the needle to the back at B and emerge within the opening. Ensure the thread is under the tip of the needle.

3 Pull the thread through loosely.

4 Take the needle from left to right behind the previous stitch. Ensure the thread is under the tip of the needle.

5 Pull the thread through firmly.

6 Continue working stitches in the same manner until reaching the right hand side of the opening.

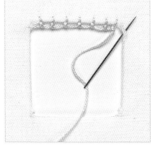

7 Take the needle from back to front through the edging on the right hand side.

8 Pull the thread through. Work 2–3 overcast stitches down the right hand edge.

9 Take the needle from top to bottom behind the last loop in the previous row. Ensure the thread is under the tip of the needle.

10 Pull the thread through loosely.

11 Take the needle from right to left behind the previous stitch. Ensure the thread is under the tip of the needle.

12 Pull the thread through firmly.

## SIDE STITCH – SINGLE *CONTINUED*

13 Continue working stitches across the row in the same manner, working one stitch into each loop of the previous row.

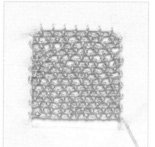

14 Continue working rows of stitches until the opening is filled.

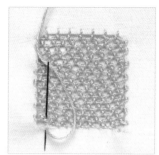

15 Anchor the loops of the last row to the lower edge of the fabric with tiny couching stitches.

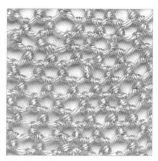

16 After the last stitch, secure on the back.

## SIDE STITCH – DOUBLE

1 Secure the thread on the back of the fabric and bring it to the front at A.

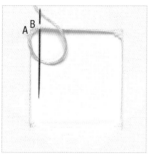

2 Take the needle to the back at B and emerge within the opening. Ensure the thread is under the tip of the needle.

3 Pull the thread through loosely.

4 Continue working stitches across the row in the same manner.

5 Take the needle from back to front through the edging on the right hand side and work 3–4 overcast stitches.

6 Take the needle from top to bottom behind the last loop in the previous row. Ensure the thread is under the tip of the needle.

7 Pull the thread through loosely.

8 Work a second detached blanket stitch into the same loop and pull it tight.

# SIDE STITCH – DOUBLE *CONTINUED*

9 Take the needle from right to left behind the loop of thread below the previous detached blanket stitches. Ensure the thread is under the tip of the needle.

10 Pull the thread through firmly.

11 Work a second stitch in the same manner.

12 Repeat steps 6–11 in the next loop to the left.

13 Continue working stitches in the same manner until reaching the left hand side of the opening.

14 Take the needle from back to front through the edging on the left hand side and work 3–4 overcast stitches.

15 Take the needle from top to bottom behind the first loop in the previous row. Ensure the thread is under the tip of the needle.

16 Pull the thread through loosely.

17 Work a second detached blanket stitch into the same loop and pull the thread firmly.

18 Take the needle from left to right behind the loop of thread below the previous detached blanket stitches. Ensure the thread is under the tip of the needle.

19 Pull the thread through firmly.

20 Work a second stitch in the same manner.

## SIDE STITCH – DOUBLE *CONTINUED*

**21** Continue working stitches across the row in the same manner.

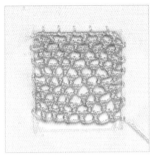

**22** Continue working rows of stitches back and forth across the opening until it is filled.

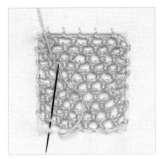

**23** Anchor the loops of the last row to the lower edge of the fabric with tiny couching stitches.

**24** After the last stitch, secure on the back.

# SPANISH POINT STITCH

**1** Secure the thread on the back of the fabric and bring it to the front at A.

**2** Loop the thread to the right in a counterclockwise direction.

**3** Take the needle to the back at B and emerge within the opening. Take the tip of the needle from front to back through the loop.

**4** Carefully pull the thread through.

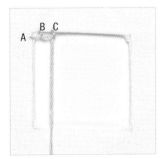

**5** Repeat steps 2–4 taking the needle to the back at C to form a second stitch.

**6** Continue working stitches across the row in the same manner.

**7** Take the needle from back to front through the edging on the right. Work 2–3 over-cast stitches down the edge.

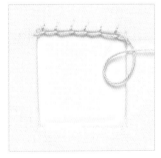

**8** Loop the thread to the left in a clockwise direction.

# SPANISH POINT STITCH *CONTINUED*

9 Take the needle from top to bottom behind the last loop in the previous row and then from front to back through the new loop.

10 Pull the thread through.

11 Repeat steps 8–10 in the next loop of the previous row.

12 Continue working stitches in the same manner until reaching the left hand side of the opening.

13 Take the needle from back to front through the edging on the left hand side and work 2–3 overcast stitches.

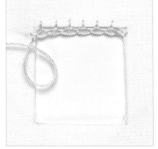

14 Loop the thread to the right in a counterclockwise direction.

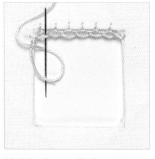

15 Take the needle from top to bottom behind the first loop in the previous row and then from front to back through the new loop.

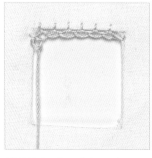

16 Pull the thread through.

17 Continue working stitches across the row in the same manner.

18 Continue working rows of stitches back and forth across the opening until it is filled.

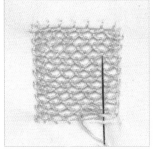

19 Anchor the loops of the last row to the lower edge of the fabric with tiny couching stitches.

20 After the last stitch, secure on the back.

# STEM STITCH

1 Draw a line on the fabric. Secure the thread on the back and bring it to the front at A.

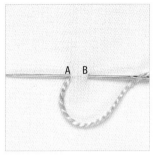

2 With the thread below the needle, take the needle to the back at B and emerge at A.

3 Pull the thread through to complete the first stitch.

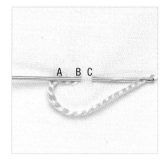

4 Again with the thread below the needle, take the needle to the back at C and emerge at B.

5 Pull the thread through to complete the second stitch.

6 Continue working stitches in the same manner, always keeping the thread below the needle.

7 To finish, take the needle to the back for the last stitch.

8 Pull the thread through and secure on the back.

# STRAIGHT STITCH

1 Secure the thread on the back of the fabric and bring it to the front at A.

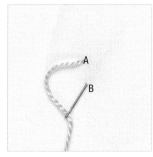

2 Take the needle to the back at B.

3 Pull the thread through and secure on the back.

4 Several straight stitches worked together.

# TRAILING STITCH

1  Position the laid threads for the padding on the front of the fabric.

2  Secure a couching thread on the back. Bring it to the front near one end, angling the needle from under the threads.

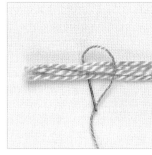

3  Pull the thread through. Take the needle to the back on the opposite side, again angling the needle under the threads.

4  Pull the thread through. Continue in the same manner. Place stitches at approx 5–10mm (³⁄₁₆–³⁄₈") intervals.

5  Take the ends of the laid threads to the back of the fabric and secure.

6  Secure a new thread on the back. Work overcast stitches over the threads, angling the needle as before (see page 15).

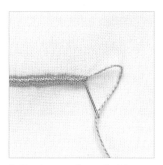

7  Continue to the end of the laid threads. To finish, take the needle to the back behind the end of the laid threads.

8  Pull the thread through and secure on the back.

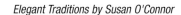

*Elegant Traditions by Susan O'Connor*

29

# Broderie Anglaise

Also known as eyelet embroidery, eyelet ruffling, Swiss embroidery, Madeira work, Scotch hole.

Broderie anglaise is French for 'English embroidery', a simple form of white on white cutwork that is characterised by the extensive use of eyelets, pierced and cut, and shaped blanket stitched edges.

Worked with soft, mercerised cotton thread on cambric, broderie anglaise designs consist of formalised patterns made up of series of round and oval holes. The holes are outlined in running stitch then tightly overcast or finished with blanket stitch. Although delicate in appearance, this style of embroidery is particularly robust and many beautiful examples have survived repeated washing and pressing in excellent condition.

Broderie anglaise became very popular in the late 18th and throughout the 19th centuries and was used to decorate babies' dresses, children's frocks, camisoles and caps as well as endless lengths that were stitched to trim the hems of petticoats, nightgowns and drawers.

## HISTORY

The origins of broderie anglaise are unclear and there are several theories on the matter. One theory suggests that it had its beginnings in Czechoslovakia and was brought to England in the 9th century. Another school of thought puts forward the theory that it evolved alongside Ayrshire embroidery in the 1800s.

Whatever its origins, by the 1860s it had usurped Ayrshire as the most fashionable embroidery style and was used extensively on ladies' and children's clothes plus household linens.

Early examples from the late 18th century used eyelets exclusively to create the design and no other embroidery stitches were employed.

Flowers and leaves were formed from small round and oval eyelets and even the stems of the flowers and veins of the leaves were worked in a succession of diminishing overcast holes. This technique meant that designs were limited and the work had a delightful simplicity.

Later examples utilised additional stitches such as satin and stem and this reduced the time needed to complete the stitching but changed the character of both the design and the work. With the addition of these new stitches came a new name and the embroidery became known as Swiss work.

Like Ayrshire embroidery, broderie anglaise was worked extensively by women outworkers as a way to supplement the family income.

*Eyelet cuff, circa mid 1800s*

"It is strange that after a lapse of nearly ten years, a perfect furore for English embroidery should obtain. The title of broderie anglaise is given to all kinds of openwork embroidery (in distinction from satin stitch embroidery) whether of Swiss, Scotch, Irish or really English production."

*The Milliner, Dressmaker and Warehousemen's Gazette, August 1871*

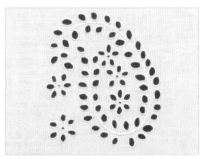

*Sample, contemporary*

Initially designs were hand drawn or printed onto paper then traced onto the fabric but eventually fabric could be purchased with the design already printed on. When transfer printing was developed it was an ideal medium for promoting eyelet designs.

Broderie anglaise enjoyed its greatest period of popularity during the Victorian era (1837–1901), a time when industrial advances and changes in fashion made embroidered ornamentation very popular. In contrast to the endless hours of badly paid piece-work endured by women struggling to keep their families fed, affluent Victorian ladies would gather in the drawing room to stitch and gossip. Being small in scale and repetitive, broderie anglaise was ideal for these occasions.

As embroidery machines were developed and refined they assumed the role of the outworker and hand work was relegated to the realm of the amateur embroiderer.

The popularity of broderie anglaise has fluctuated over the years but each era seems to find a place for it, a testament to its classic appeal. It experienced a resurgence in popularity in the 1950s when it was used on both dresses and underwear. Brigitte Bardot even wore a wedding dress of gingham with broderie anglaise trim when she married Jacques Charrier in 1959.

## MATERIALS

### Fabrics

Fine linens and cottons such as lawn and poplin are excellent choices for broderie anglaise. The fabric needs to be finely woven so it will not fray easily and needs to have enough body to support the embroidery. Avoid fabrics that are very tightly woven as it will be difficult to open holes with an awl or stiletto.

Launder the fabric before using to pre-shrink it and press and starch before applying the design.

### Threads

Broderie anglaise should be worked with a single strand of soft cotton thread and broder spécial and floche are ideal. Broder spécial is a four ply, non-divisible thread that comes in six sizes, 12 (coarse), 16, 20, 25, 30 and 40 (fine). Floche is a five ply, non-divisible thread most commonly available in size 16. Stranded cotton can also be used but it is not as strong. Try stranded silk and linen thread for a variation in finish. Choose a weight of thread that is suitable for the weight of the fabric being used.

### Needles

Sharp and crewel needles are both suitable for working broderie anglaise.

Floche and broder spécial are round threads so choose a needle with an eye large enough so that the thread does not untwist as it passes through.

### Other

Broderie anglaise is best worked in the hand so that the fabric is more easily manipulated and the eyelet overcasting stitches can be pulled firmly.

A stiletto or dressmaker's awl is essential for piercing the fabric for small eyelets. Take care to divide the threads rather than breaking them when piercing a hole in the fabric. Small, sharp, pointed scissors are also necessary for cutting eyelets, blanket stitch edges and trimming away stray fibres.

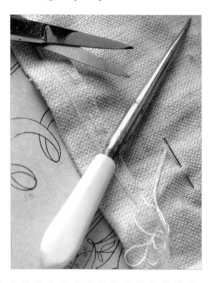

*Edging, circa mid 1800s*

### STITCHES FOR BRODERIE ANGLAISE

Blanket stitch
   *padded, scallops*
Eyelets
   *pierced, cut*
   *shaded, flower*
   *linked*

Overcast stitch
Running stitch
Satin stitch
   *flat, slightly padded*
   *highly padded*
Stem stitch

# BLANKET STITCH

1 Secure the thread on the back of the fabric and bring it to the front at A.

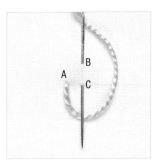

2 Take the needle to the back at B and emerge at C. Ensure the thread is under the tip of the needle.

3 Pull the thread through until it lies snugly against the emerging thread but does not distort the fabric.

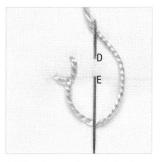

4 Take the needle to the back at D and emerge at E. Ensure the thread lies under the tip of the needle.

5 Pull the thread through as before.

6 Continue working stitches in the same manner.

7 To finish, take the needle to the back of the fabric just over the last loop.

8 Pull the thread through and secure on the back.

# BLANKET STITCH – PADDED

1 Mark the area to be covered by the blanket stitch onto your fabric.

2 Fill the area to be covered with rows of running stitch at right angles to the direction of the blanket stitches.

3 Alternatively, fill the area to be covered with rows of chain stitch.

## BLANKET STITCH – PADDED *CONTINUED*

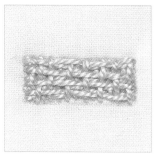

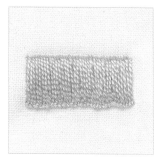

**4** If the area needs to be highly raised, work rows of darning within the outline.

**5** Continue adding layers of darning until the area is the desired height.

**6** Cover the padding with blanket stitch, following the instructions on page 32.

# BLANKET STITCH – SCALLOPS

**1** Work running stitch along the design lines.

**2** Fill the space with rows of running stitches, making them as long as possible on the front of the work. Work a second layer if desired.

**3** Bring the thread to the surface on the lower line.

**4** Take the needle to the back outside the upper line and emerge just below the lower line.

**5** Pull the thread through. Continue working in this manner along the line.

*The Pillow from Monograms – The Art of Embroidered Letters by Susan O'Connor*

# BLANKET STITCH – JOINING A NEW THREAD

1 Work to the end of the thread. Take the needle off the thread and leave it hanging.

2 Bring the new thread to the surface on the lower line next to the hanging thread.

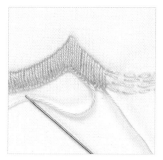

3 Work five or six blanket stitches. Re-thread the end.

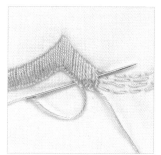

4 Take the needle under the bead of the next stitch and into the fabric.

5 Finish the thread securely between the design lines.

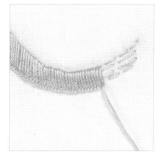

6 Continue working with the new thread.

## Early whitework

The earliest examples of whitework have been found in Coptic tombs in Egypt.

*Broderie anglasie seed patterms, circa mid 1800s*

# EYELET – PIERCED

*These tiny, round eyelets are less than 5mm (¼") in diameter.*

**1** Mark the position of the eyelet with a tiny circle on the right side of the fabric.

**2** Leaving a short tail, work running stitch around the circle.

**3** When reaching the first stitch, take the last stitch through the first stitch, splitting it.

**4** Pull the thread through. Pierce the centre of the circle with an awl, carefully separating the fibres rather than breaking them.

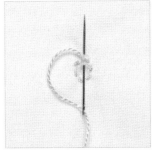

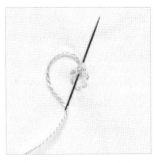

**5** Bring the thread to the front just outside the running stitch.

**6** Take the needle through the hole and emerge on the outer edge.

**7** Pull the thread through.

**8** Take the needle through the hole and emerge alongside the previous stitch.

**9** Pull the thread through. Continue working overcast stitches in the same manner, turning the fabric as you work.

**10** When the edge is completely covered take the needle to the back through the hole.

**11** To secure, take the thread behind the overcast stitches on the back.

**12** Carefully re-pierce the hole with the awl to ensure it is round.

# EYELET – CUT

1 Draw a circle on the right side of the fabric to mark the position of the eyelet.

2 Leaving a short tail work running stitch around the circle.

3 When reaching the first stitch, take the last stitch through the first stitch, splitting it.

4 Pull the thread through and bring it to the front just outside the running stitch.

5 Using small sharp scissors, cut the fabric within the circle as shown. Take care not to cut the thread.

6 Fold the flaps of fabric to the back away from the centre and finger press.

7 Take the needle through the hole and emerge on the outer edge.

8 Pull the thread through.

9 Take the needle through the hole and emerge alongside the previous stitch.

10 Pull the thread through. Continue working overcast stitches in the same manner, turning the fabric as you work.

11 When the edge is completely covered take the needle to the back through the hole.

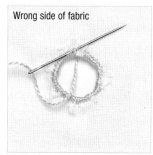

12 To secure, take the thread behind the overcast stitches on the back.

# EYELET – CUT *CONTINUED*

13 Trim away the excess fabric on the wrong side of the eyelet.

14 Completed eyelet.

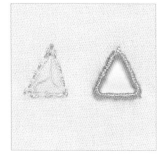

15 Work triangular eyelets in the same manner, cutting the fabric as shown. Lengthen the overcasting stitches on the corners.

16 Work petal eyelets in the same manner, cutting fabric as shown. Lengthen the overcasting stitches on the point.

# EYELET – SHADED

1 Draw a circle on the right side of the fabric to mark the position of the eyelet. Draw the shaded area around half of the circle.

2 Leaving a short tail, work running stitch around the shaded area and the first half of the circle.

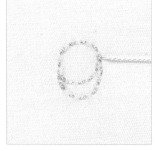

3 When reaching the first stitch, take a stitch through it, splitting it. Work running stitch around the remainder of the circle.

4 Fill the shaded area with several rows of running stitch for padding, finishing with the thread on the front.

5 Using small sharp scissors, cut the fabric within the circle as shown. Take care not to cut the thread.

6 Fold the flaps of fabric to the back away from the centre and finger press.

7 Take the thread to the back and emerge just beyond the outline.

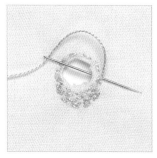

8 Take the needle through the hole and emerge on the outer edge.

# EYELET – SHADED *CONTINUED*

**9** Pull the thread through.

**10** Take the needle through the hole and emerge alongside the previous stitch.

**11** Pull the thread through. Continue working overcast stitches in the same manner, turning the fabric as you work.

**12** When the edge is completely covered take the needle to the back through the hole.

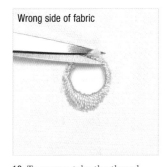

**13** To secure, take the thread behind the overcast stitches on the back. Trim away the excess fabric on the wrong side of the eyelet.

**14** Completed shaded eyelet.

**15** Shaded eyelet worked with blanket stitch instead of overcast stitch.

**16** Shaded eyelet worked with blanket stitch around the shaded area and overcast stitch around the remainder.

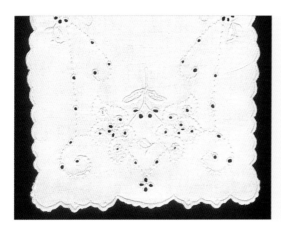

## Normandy bonnets

During the 14th century, in France's Normandy, it became the custom to present every bride with a whitework bonnet. These fine linen bonnets, which were exclusively the domain of married women, were embroidered on various parts. The mainly floral motifs utilised blanket stitch, chain stitch and stem stitch as well as numerous pulled thread stitches.

*Handkerchief sachet*

# EYELETS – LINKED

*Rows of eyelets worked this way are stronger than eyelets worked individually.*

1 Draw a series of circles on the right side of the fabric to mark the positions of the eyelets.

2 Leaving a short tail, work running stitch around one half of the first circle.

3 Work running stitch around the opposite half of the next circle.

4 Continue working running stitches around half of each circle, alternating between the upper and lower halves.

5 Work running stitches back across the remaining halves of the circles in the same manner.

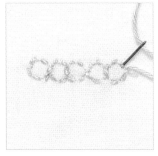

6 When reaching the beginning, take the last stitch through the first stitch, splitting it.

7 Pierce each circle with the awl.

8 Bring the thread to the front just outside the running stitch on the first circle.

9 Work overcast stitch around one half of the circle as shown.

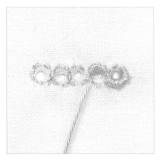

10 Avoid stitching the area where the two circles meet. Work overcast stitch around the opposite half of the next circle.

11 Continue working over-cast stitch around half of each circle, alternating between the upper and lower halves.

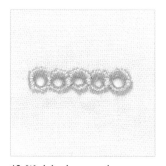

12 Work back across the remaining halves of the circles including the area where the two circles meet. End off within the stitching on the back.

# RUNNING STITCH

 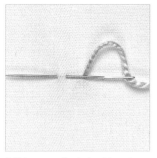 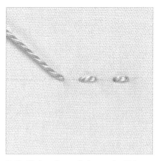 

**1** Draw a line on the fabric. Secure the thread on the back and bring it to the front on the right hand end of the line.

**2** Take a small stitch, skimming the needle beneath the fabric along the line.

**3** Pull the thread through. Take another stitch in the same manner as before. Ensure the stitches are the same length.

**4** Continue to the end of the line. Take the needle to the back for the last stitch. Pull through and secure on the back.

*The Christening Shawl from Monograms – The Art of Embroidered Letters by Susan O'Connor*

# Candlewicking

## Also known as tufting, Bolton work

*There are two forms of candlewicking – one woven and the other embroidered. In embroidered candlewicking, colonial knots dominate although French knots and other surface embroidery stitches can be used. These simple embroideries have a wonderful tactile quality and characteristically contain clean design lines and large amounts of blank space.*

## HISTORY

The origins of candlewicking are somewhat muddled, but in its most common form, this style of embroidery is closely linked to the ingenious colonial women who settled in America. It is thought that these women took the knowledge of traditional English tufted quilts with them to their new homes and with the meagre supplies they had at hand – unbleached muslin and the thick cotton wicking intended for candlemaking – created decorative bed covers. Although candlewicking is now heavily associated with surface knots, these early examples featured tufting that was created by working running stitch over a turkey quill or small bone, leaving a loop once the object was removed. These loops were cut and the fabric washed, shrinking it to secure the tufts into the fabric. This type of tufting is often referred to as turkey work.

This style of candlewicking was worked with a thick embroidery needle with two eyes, one above the other, so that two threads could be worked at the same time.

Another method involved couching lengths of cotton cord to the base fabric with small stitches, then cutting between the stitches to create the tufts.

There was also a woven form of tufted candlewicking where the pattern was created by inserting reeds into the flat woven surface to create loops. Cotton thread was then wound around the loops and the reeds were removed. This woven candlewicking is thought to precede the embroidered form.

Gradually surface stitches were introduced and superceded the tufting as a way to create the textured surface that was so prized. Candlewicking was washed but not pressed as the crinkled ground is typical of this work.

Colonial women often used quilting patterns for designs, working the design lines with knots rather than running stitches. Designs were often shared amongst families and ingenious methods were found for transferring designs. New fabric would be placed over a borrowed quilt and a cast iron cooking pot would be rubbed lightly over the surface, leaving black marks over the stitched areas.

With the passing of pioneer days, the popularity of candlewicking waned. However the 1980s saw a revival of its popularity in South Africa and Australia as well as in America.

*Grace by Yvette Stanton*

*Timelines by Yvette Stanton*

## MATERIALS

### Fabrics

Sturdy unbleached cotton muslin (calico) is still widely available and is ideal if you wish to create an authentic copy of pioneer work. Use fabric that has not been pre-shrunk and when the embroidery is finished, dip the work in hot water. This will cause the fabric to shrink slightly, tightening the stitches and giving a soft puckered surface to the work that is typical of this style.

Most medium weight, even weave cotton fabrics would also be suitable, as would very lightweight cotton canvas.

### Threads

Special candlewicking threads are manufactured but may be difficult to find. Choose alternatives with a matte surface, such as knitting and crochet cottons or DMC soft cotton thread. Traditional candlewicks were much thicker than most contemporary embroidery threads, some being equivalent in weight to a double knitting or sport weight yarn. Use a double thread as required. Avoid lustrous threads as they will not give an authentic finish.

### Needles

Choose a chenille or crewel needle with an eye large enough to accommodate the thread. When working knot stitches, a long darner will be useful.

### Other

Place the fabric in an embroidery hoop before beginning to work. A stand or seat frame is ideal as both hands are then free to work, as many candlewicking stitches require two hands.

## STITCHES FOR CANDLEWICKING

| | | |
|---|---|---|
| Back stitch | Detached chain | Outline stitch |
| Blanket stitch | *single, double* | Running stitch |
| *closed, up and down* | Feather stitch | Satin stitch |
| Cable stitch | Fishbone stitch | Split stitch |
| Colonial knot | Fly stitch | Stem stitch |
| Coral stitch | French knot | Straight stitch |
| Couching | Herringbone stitch | Trellis stitch |

# BACK STITCH

1 Secure the thread on the back of the fabric and bring it to the front at A, a short distance from the right hand end.

2 Take the needle to the back at the right hand end (B). Emerge at C.

3 Pull the thread through to complete the first stitch.

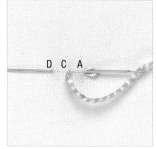

4 Take the needle to the back at A, using the same hole in the fabric as before. Emerge at D, on the other side of C.

5 Pull the thread through to complete the second stitch.

6 Continue working stitches in the same manner.

7 To end off, take the needle to the back through the hole at the beginning of the previous stitch.

8 Pull the thread through and secure on the back.

# BLANKET STITCH – CLOSED

1 Secure the thread on the back of the fabric and bring it to the front at A.

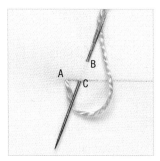

2 Take the needle to the back at B and emerge at C, ensuring it is angled as shown. Ensure the thread is under the tip of the needle.

3 Pull the thread through until it lies snugly against the emerging thread but does not distort the fabric.

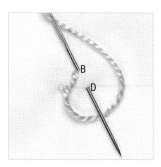

4 Take the needle to the back at B again and emerge at D, ensuring it is angled as shown. Ensure the thread is under the tip of the needle.

5 Pull the thread through as before.

6 Continue working stitches in the same manner.

7 To finish, take the needle to the back of the fabric just over the last loop.

8 Pull the thread through and secure on the back.

# BLANKET STITCH – UP AND DOWN

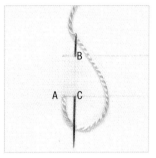

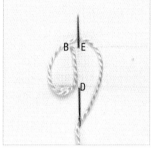

1 Secure the thread on the back of the fabric and bring it to the front at A.

2 Take the needle to the back at B and emerge at C. Ensure the thread is under the tip of the needle.

3 Pull the thread through until it lies snugly against the emerging thread but does not distort the fabric.

4 Take the needle to the back at D and emerge at E. Ensure the thread is under the tip of the needle.

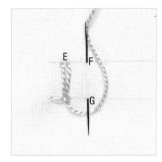

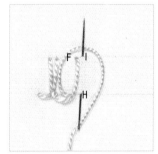

5 Pull the thread through, pulling it away from you.

6 Pull the thread towards you. A small straight stitch will lie across the vertical stitches.

7 Take the needle to the back at F and emerge at G. Ensure the thread is under the tip of the needle.

8 Pull the thread through as before. Take the needle to the back at H and emerge at I. Ensure the thread is under the tip of the needle.

## BLANKET STITCH – UP AND DOWN *CONTINUED*

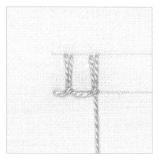

9 Pull the thread through as before, pulling it away from you and then towards you.

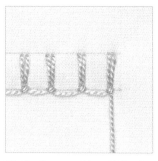

10 Continue working stitches in the same manner.

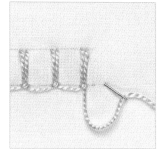

11 To finish, take the needle to the back of the fabric as shown.

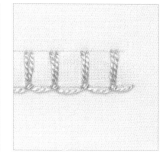

12 Pull the thread through and secure on the back.

# CABLE STITCH

1 Secure the thread on the back of the fabric and bring it to the front at A.

2 With the thread below the needle, take the needle from C to B. B is halfway between A and C.

3 Pull the thread through.

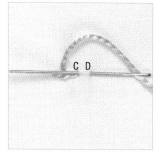

4 With the thread above the needle, take the needle from D to C.

5 Pull the thread through.

6 Continue working stitches in the same manner, alter-nating the thread above and below the needle.

7 Take the needle to the back for the last stitch.

8 Pull the thread through and secure on the back.

# COLONIAL KNOT

1 Secure the thread on the back of the fabric and bring it to the front at the position for the knot.

2 Hook the needle under the thread where it emerges from the fabric.

3 Take the thread over the tip of the needle to form a loop. Shorten the loop.

4 Take the thread under the tip of the needle to form a figure eight around the needle.

5 Take the tip of the needle to the back of the fabric approximately two fabric threads away from where it first emerged.

6 Pull the wraps firmly against the fabric.

7 Keeping the thread taut, push the needle through the knot to the back of the fabric.

8 Hold the knot and loop on the fabric and continue to pull the thread through.

9 Pull until the loop disappears. Secure the thread on the back.

## Elizabethan embroidery

During Elizabethan times, whitework embroidery was often used for ruffs and undergarments. It could incorporate drawn thread work, cutwork and faggoting. Many of the large ruffs that looked like lace were in fact whitework.

# CORAL STITCH - SINGLE

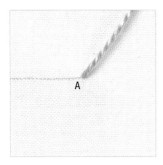

1 Mark a line on the fabric. Secure the thread on the back and bring it to the front at A, on the right hand end of the line.

2 Hold the thread along the line and loop it to the right.

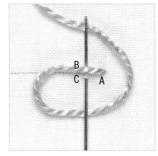

3 Take the needle to the back at B, just above the thread. Emerge at C, just below the thread.

4 Begin to gently pull the thread through.

5 Pull until a knot forms.

6 Lay the thread along the line again and loop it as in step 2.

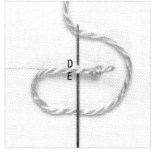

7 Take the needle to the back at D and emerge at E. Ensure the loop is under the tip of the needle.

8 Begin to gently pull the thread through as before.

9 Pull the thread through as before to form a second knot.

10 Continue working stitches to the end of the line in the same manner.

11 To finish, take the needle to the back, just after the last knot.

12 Pull the thread through and secure on the back.

# COUCHING

1 Secure the foundation thread on the back of the fabric and bring it to the front at A. Lay the thread on the fabric.

2 Secure the couching thread on the back of the fabric and bring it to the front just above the laid thread.

3 Take the needle over the laid thread and to the back of the fabric.

4 Pull the thread through to form the first couching stitch.

5 Bring the thread to the front just above the laid thread.

6 Continue working stitches in the same manner for the required distance.

7 Take the couching thread to the back and secure.

8 Take the laid thread to the back of the fabric and secure.

# DETACHED CHAIN

1 Secure the thread on the back of the fabric and bring it to the front at A. This is the base of the stitch.

2 Hold the thread to the left.

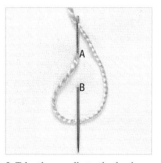

3 Take the needle to the back at A, through the same hole in the fabric. Emerge at B. Loop the thread under the tip of the needle.

## Toledo

Toledo, a province in south-central Spain, was once famous for the beautiful whitework embroidery it employed to decorate men's shirts.

## DETACHED CHAIN *CONTINUED*

4 Pull the thread through. The tighter you pull, the thinner the stitch will become.

5 To finish, take the needle to the back just over the loop.

6 Pull the thread through and secure on the back.

## DETACHED CHAIN – DOUBLE

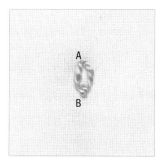

1 Secure the thread on the back and work a single detached chain from A–B following the instructions above.

2 Bring the thread to the front at C, just above A. Hold the thread to the left.

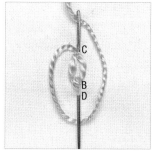

3 Take the needle to the back at C, through the same hole in the fabric. Emerge at D, just below B. Loop the thread under the tip of the needle.

4 Pull the thread through until the loop lies alongside the outer edge of the first loop.

5 To finish, take the needle to the back just over the loop.

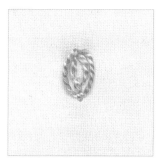

6 Pull the thread through and secure on the back.

## Kappies

Dutch settlers to South Africa brought their rich tradition of embroidery with them. Women continued to embroider items of clothing such as blouses, aprons and hats in the style of their homeland.

The African landscape, with its unique flora, gradually began to have an influence on the subjects of embroidery.

One particular item that reflected this was the kappie – a bonnet with a wide poke brim and back flap that was worn by both women and girls. Kappies were made of fine white cotton and richly and intricately embroidered. They often incorporated quilting and cutwork as well as surface embroidery.

# FEATHER STITCH – SINGLE

1 Bring the needle to the front at A. This will be the left hand side of the stitch.

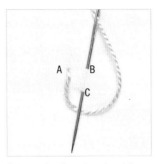

2 Loop the thread to the right and take the needle from B to C. Ensure the thread is under the tip of the needle.

3 Pull the thread through in a downward movement and hold firmly with your thumb.

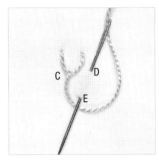

4 Again, loop the thread to the right and take the needle from D to E. Ensure the thread is under the tip of the needle.

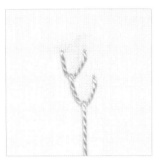

5 Pull the thread through in the same manner as before.

6 Loop the thread to the left and take the needle from F to G. Ensure the thread is under the tip of the needle.

7 Pull the thread through. Continue working stitches in the same manner.

8 To finish, take the needle to the back of the fabric just over the last loop. Pull the thread through and secure.

*Antique tea cloth, late 19th century*

*Pulpit cover, early 20th century*

# FEATHER STITCH – DOUBLE

1 Rule three parallel lines. Secure the thread on the back of the fabric and bring it to the front at A.

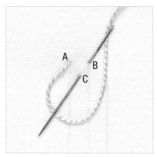

2 Take the needle to the back at B and emerge at C, halfway between and slightly lower than A and B. Loop the thread to the right and under the needle.

3 Pull the thread through in a downward movement.

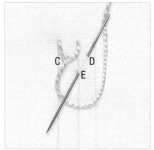

4 Keeping the thread taut, loop it to the right. Take the needle from D to E, ensuring the loop is under the tip of the needle.

5 Pull the thread through in a downward movement.

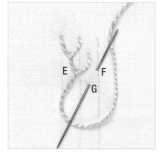

6 Keeping the thread taut, loop it to the right again. Take the needle from F to G. Ensure the loop is under the tip of the needle.

7 Pull the thread through as before.

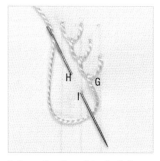

8 Loop the thread to the left. Take the needle from H to I, ensuring the loop is under the tip of the needle.

9 Pull the thread through as before. Loop the thread and take the needle from J to K.

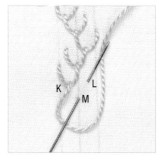

10 Pull the thread through as before. Loop the thread to the right and take the needle from L to M.

11 Pull the thread through as before. Loop the thread to the right. Take the needle from N to O and pull the thread through.

12 Continue working two stitches to the left and two to the right. Take the needle to the back just over the last loop. Pull through and secure.

# FISHBONE STITCH

1 Mark the shape and a centre line on the fabric. Secure the thread on the back and bring it to the front at A.

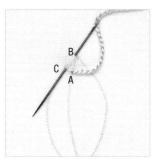

2 Take the needle from B to C. Ensure the thread is to the right of the needle.

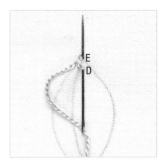

3 Pull the thread through. Loop the thread to the left and take the needle from D to E.

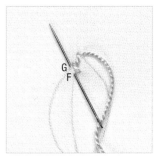

4 Pull the thread through. Take the needle from F to G. Ensure the thread is to the right of the needle.

5 Pull the thread through. Take the needle from H to I. Ensure the thread is to the left of the needle.

6 Pull the thread through. Continue working stitches in the same manner, alternating from one side to the other.

7 To finish, take the needle to the back near the centre line.

8 Pull the thread through and secure on the back.

# FLY STITCH

1 Secure the thread on the back of the fabric and bring it to the front at A. This will be the left hand side of the stitch.

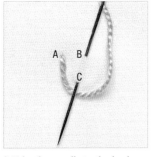

2 Take the needle to the back at B and emerge at C. Loop the thread under the tip of the needle.

3 Pull the thread until the loop lies snugly against C.

4 Take the thread to the back of the fabric below C to anchor the loop. Secure the thread on the back.

# FRENCH KNOT

1 Secure the thread on the back of the fabric and bring it to the front at the position for the knot.

2 Hold the thread firmly approximately 3cm (1⅛") from the fabric.

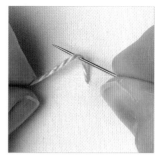

3 Take the thread over the needle, ensuring the needle points away from the fabric.

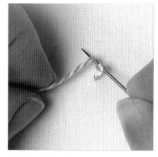

4 Wrap the thread around the needle. Keeping the thread taut, turn the tip of the needle towards the fabric.

5 Take the tip of the needle to the back of the fabric approximately 1–2 fabric threads away from where it emerged.

6 Slide the knot down the needle onto the fabric. Pull the thread until the knot is firmly around the needle.

7 Push the needle through the fabric and pull the thread through.

8 Pull until the loop of thread completely disappears. Secure the thread on the back.

# HERRINGBONE STITCH

1 Rule two parallel lines. Bring the thread to the front at A, on the left hand side of the lower line.

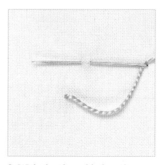

2 With the thread below the needle, take the needle from right to left on the upper line as shown.

3 Pull the thread through.

4 With the thread above the needle, take the needle from right to left on the lower line.

## HERRINGBONE STITCH *CONTINUED*

5 Pull the thread through. With the thread below the needle, take the needle from right to left on the upper line.

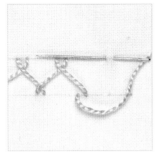

6 Pull the thread through. Continue working stitches in the same manner, alternating between the two lines.

7 To finish, take the needle to the back of the fabric for the last stitch.

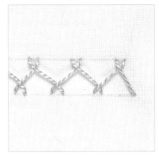

8 Pull the thread through and secure on the back.

# SPLIT STITCH

1 Draw a line on the fabric. Secure the thread on the back and bring it to the front at A, on the right hand end.

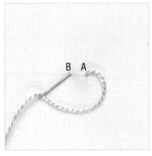

2 Take the needle to the back at B, a short distance away.

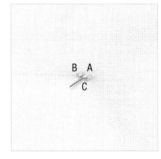

3 Pull the thread through. Bring the needle to the front at C, splitting the thread in the middle of the first stitch.

4 Pull the thread through.

5 Take the needle to the back at D.

6 Pull the thread through. Bring the needle to the front at B, splitting the thread in the middle of the second stitch.

7 Pull the thread through. Continue working stitches in the same manner.

8 Secure the thread on the back.

54

# TRELLIS STITCH

1 Outline the shape on the fabric. Secure the thread on the back and bring it to the front at A.

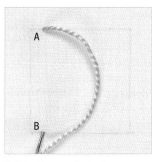

2 Take the needle to the back at B.

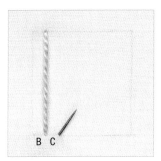

3 Pull the thread through. Emerge at C, the required distance from B.

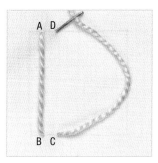

4 Pull the thread through. Take the needle to the back at D on the opposite side.

5 Pull the thread through. Continue working parallel straight stitches to the end of the shape. Ensure they are evenly spaced.

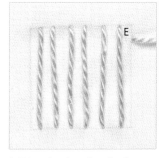

6 Bring the thread to the front at E to begin the second layer of straight stitches.

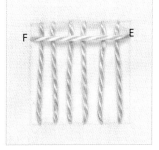

7 Take the needle to the back at F. Pull the thread through to form a straight stitch at right angles to the previous layer of stitches.

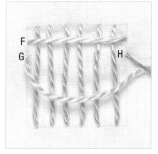

8 Bring the thread to the front at G. Take the needle to the back at H, directly opposite G.

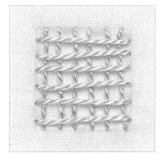

9 Continue working parallel stitches in the same manner to the end of the shape. Secure the thread on the back.

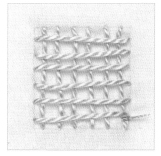

10 Secure a new thread on the back near the right hand side. Bring the needle to the front just below and to the left of one intersection.

11 Pull the thread through. Take the needle to the back just above and to the right of the intersection.

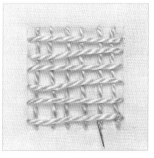

12 Pull the thread through and emerge just below and to the left of the next intersection.

# TRELLIS STITCH *CONTINUED*

 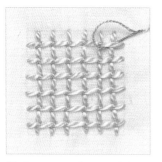  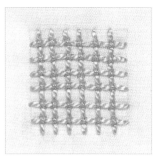

**13** Anchor the intersection as before and continue across the row in the same manner.

**14** Continue anchoring all the intersections in the same manner, taking particular care to ensure the stitches all lie in the same direction.

**15** After working the last anchoring stitch, secure on the back.

**16** As an alternative, anchor each intersection with a small cross stitch.

*Venetian cutwork, contemporary*

*Renaissance cutwork, contemporary*

# Carrickmacross embroidery

## Also known as the Flowerin', the sewings, the parcellings

Often described as a lace, Carrickmacross is, in reality, a form of embroidery onto a net ground. The design is transferred to a sheet of paper then a piece of cotton net is placed over it. This is tacked to the design, working from the centre outwards. A layer of fine cotton muslin is then laid over the net and is tacked down, again working from the centre outwards. The design is sewn through both fabric layers by couching a thicker thread around the outlines with a finer thread. Characteristic picots are worked into the outline. The paper with the design is then removed. Unwanted areas of the top fabric are then carefully cut away to reveal the lace ground and filling stitches are worked into the net. Both layers can also be cut away in some areas and the open spaces are supported by embroidered bars or 'brides'. Alternatively, the muslin shapes are cut and the edges are overcast, then the piece is applied to the net ground. The overall effect is that of a delicately beautiful appliqué 'lace'.

### HISTORY

Carrickmacross embroidery is named after the town in Ireland where it originated in the early 1820s. In 1801 a machine was invented to manufacture net and this revived the interest in net embroidery. The work came about when Mrs Grey Porter of Donaghmoyne, purchased lace in Italy on her honeymoon. She and her sewing maid, Ann Steadman, taught themselves the appliqué technique by copying the Italian designs. Mrs Porter could see the potential of a cottage industry and the opportunity for local women to earn money from selling their work.

The skill soon spread throughout the district and a school was established to teach women, mainly farmers' wives who sought outwork to supplement their failing farm incomes. The area around Carrickmacross was particularly hard hit by the Great Famine and the town, with a population of less than three thousand people, lost one third of its inhabitants. The finished pieces were sold to middle men who then sold them to the upper classes or for export.

*Detail of christening gown, courtsey of the museum of The Embroiderers' Guild of South Australia*

"That the Irish have loved the arts of the embroiderer from very early times is evident from references in the epic tales of the pre-Christian Cuchulain cycle in which Cuchulain's wife, Emer, is renowned, among other attributes, for her 'gift of embroidery and needlework'."

*Nellie Ó Cléirigh, Carrickmacross Lace*

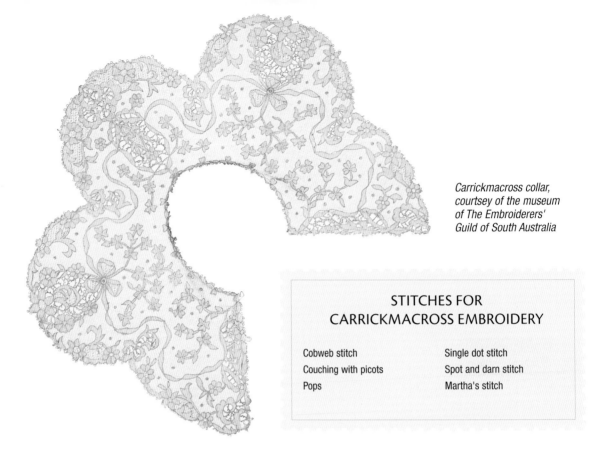

*Carrickmacross collar,
courtsey of the museum
of The Embroiderers'
Guild of South Australia*

## STITCHES FOR
## CARRICKMACROSS EMBROIDERY

| | |
|---|---|
| Cobweb stitch | Single dot stitch |
| Couching with picots | Spot and darn stitch |
| Pops | Martha's stitch |

By 1860, embroidered pieces from the district were being exhibited in Paris, Milan, London and North America. The work was used mainly on lingerie, collars, cuffs and baby wear. The name Carrickmacross was not used until 1872.

The popularity of the technique waned towards the end of the 19th century. It was revived by the nuns of the St Louis Convent of Carrickmacross who set up classes in 1897 to teach their students the fine embroidery. The convent is largely responsible for the continued production of the embroidery.

Carrickmacross is still made today and is heavily associated with wedding gowns and veils. On her marriage to Prince Charles, Lady Diana Spencer had ruffles of Carrickma-cross embroidery on the sleeves of her dress.

## MATERIALS

### Fabrics

Carrickmacross was trad-itionally worked with fine muslin onto a machine made cotton net. Fine muslins of the quality traditionally used are no longer manufactured but a good quality, finely woven cotton voile, batiste or organdie is suitable. Cotton net is still manufactured and is preferable to nylon as a base for the work.

### Threads

Two weights of cotton thread are required; a size 50 and a size 30 machine thread are ideal. Fine cotton crochet thread, such as Coats Mercer crochet cotton no. 60, can also be used as the thicker thread.

### Needles

Two sizes of needle are required. Use a fine sharp or crewel needle (size 10–12) for working the couching and a fine tapestry needle (size 26–28) for working the filling stitches.

### Other

Carrickmacross embroidery is worked in the hand, the paper pattern giving stability to the fabrics while the important outlines are worked.

Lacemaker's scissors, while not essential, are handy as the knob at the end of one blade prevents the net base from damage while the top layer is cut away.

# COBWEB STITCH

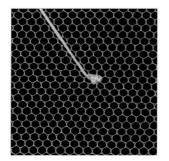

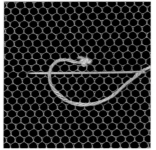

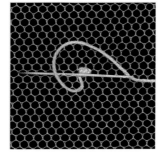

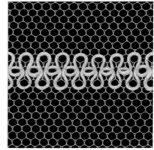

**1** Secure the thread and bring it to the front.

**2** Take the needle under two lower bars, two rows below.

**3** Pull the thread through. Take the needle under two upper bars, to the left the starting point.

**4** Continue along the row. Work the return row as a mirror image. Repeat, filling the area.

# COUCHING WITH PICOTS

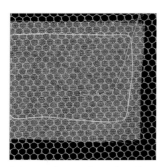

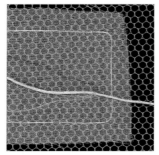

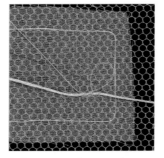

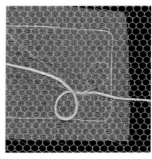

**1** Secure the couching thread in the fabric with several small running stitches along the design line.

**2** Leaving a tail, lay the thicker thread along the design line. Work the first stitch, ensuring that it slants in such a way that it sinks into the twist of the thicker thread.

**3** Continue working couching stitches to the position of the first picot.

**4** Coil the thicker thread to form a picot. Work a couching stitch to hold the loop in place.

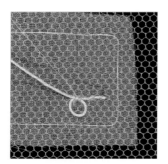

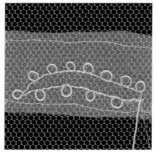

**5** Pull to adjust the picot size. Work two more couching stitches to secure. Trim away the thread tail.

**6** Continue working in this manner until the line is complete.

# MARTHA'S STITCH

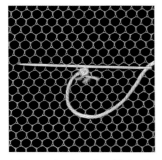

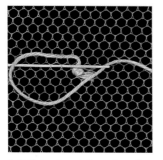

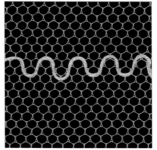

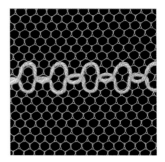

1 Secure the thread and bring it to the front. Take the needle under the upper two bars.

2 Pull the thread through and take the needle under the lower two bars to the left.

3 Pull the thread through and continue, taking the needle through the upper and then the lower pairs of bars.

4 Work the return row as a mirror image. Repeat, filling the area.

# POPS

*These quaintly named stitches are traditionally the last part of the embroidery to be worked.*
*They are used to fill in blank areas of net or to emphasise the design.*

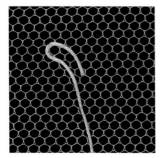

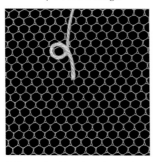

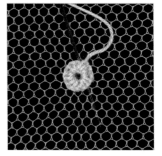

1 Leaving a small tail, work running stitches around one hole in the net.

2 Bring the thread to the surface outside the line of running stitch.

3 Working into the cental hole, embroider blanket stitch around the circle. In-corporate the tail of thread.

4 Take the thread to the back over the loop of the first stitch.

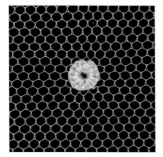

5 End the thread at the back of the work under the previously worked stitches.

*Italian Reticella, c1600s*

60

# SINGLE DOT STITCH

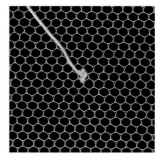

1 Secure the thread and bring it to the front.

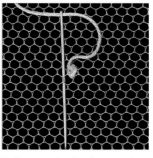

2 Oversew the first hexagon by taking the needle under the first vertical bar to the left.

3 Pull the thread through and continue oversewing the hexagons from right to left.

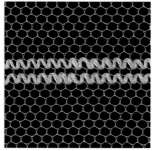

4 Leave a row of hexagons. Repeat in the opposite direction. Continue, filling the area with the required number of rows.

# SPOT AND DARN STITCH

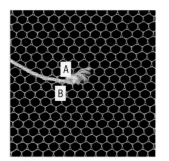

1 Secure the thread at A and bring to the front at B.

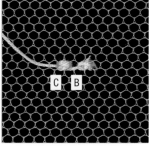

2 Work two stitches around the two bars to the right of B. Work a third stitch, emerging at C.

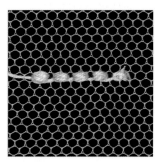

3 Continue working three stitches around each pair of bars.

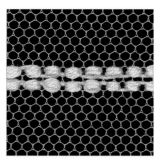

4 At the end of the row turn and darn under and over the bars of the row above. Repeat steps 1 to 4, filling the area.

# Cutwork

## Also known as opus scissum

Cutwork is a general term that encompasses a number of more specific embroidery styles. All share the basic technique of edging motifs with close stitches, then cutting away parts of the ground fabric to emphasise the design.

In some forms the stability of the remaining motifs is maintained by embroidered bars with varying levels of ornamentation.

Cutwork is regarded as the forerunner to needlemade laces and finest examples are difficult to distinguish from lace. The following are the main styles of cutwork.

### Roman cutwork

This is the simplest form of cutwork where the motifs of the design touch one another, making additional bars of stitching unnecessary. As the technique is simple, the designs are often extremely elaborate and the motifs can be further enhanced with surface stitching.

### Renaissance cutwork

The cut sections in this form of cutwork are often larger than those in Roman cutwork and are transversed with simple bars or 'brides', as they are also known. These may be woven or twisted or worked with blanket stitch. In some examples of Renaissance cutwork the motifs are filled in with flat laid stitches, giving an additional richness to the surface of the work.

### Richelieu cutwork

This is very similar to Renaissance but the bars are ornamented with thread picots, adding to the lacy appearance of the work. Richelieu also uses small detached blanket stitch rings at the intersections of branched bars.

### Venetian cutwork

This form of cutwork is characterised by heavy padding of both the blanket stitched edges and the satin stitch that is used within the design.

### Reticella cutwork

Also known as Italian cutwork, this form is characterised by the removal of threads in the fabric, leaving small squares that are filled with needlelace stitches. This form of cutwork is much more geometric in design than other forms as the cutting of the base fabric relies primarily on the weave of the fabric. The term 'reticella' was used in 1493 for cut and drawn work. Reticella is Italian and translates as 'little net' or 'mesh stitch'.

### HISTORY

Varying forms of cutwork have developed throughout Europe over the centuries and although these vary greatly in style and colour, all utilise the basic technique of removing parts of the base fabric. Regional techniques often borrow heavily from other areas but all seem to develop a distinctive style that makes them easily recognisable as belonging to a specific culture.

Fine cutwork reached its zenith in the 16th century when it was used largely for clothing and household linen. Reticella cutwork was worked extensively in Venice but is thought to have originated in Greece, on the Ionian Isles and Corfu. Magnificent examples of reticella collars and cuffs can be seen in portraits from the 16th

· · · · · · · · · · · · · · · · · · · · · · · · · · · · · · · · · · · · · · · · · · · · · · ·

"Two ruffs with rabatines of lawn cut-work made, and one ruff of lawne cutt-work unmade"

*New year's gift to Elizabeth I from Baroness Dudley*

and 17th centuries. Cutwork became so popular in England that sumptuary laws were imposed, limiting the wearing of cutwork to men who were of the title of baron or higher and to women who were married to a man who ranked no lower than a knight.

This style of cutwork eventually evolved into lace, 'punto in aria' or 'a stitch in the air' when embroiderers realised that the fabric was not necessary at all. As lace gained in popularity, cutwork fell out of favour but was to enjoy a resurgence in popularity during the Victorian era (1837–1901). Cutwork became popular again, but in a much simpler form than the intricate and exquisite reticella, and was used primarily for household linens such as doyleys and tablecloths.

Renaissance cutwork earned its name during this time as it concentrated on using designs from the Renaissance period (1400–1600).

Richelieu cutwork is named after Cardinal Richelieu (1585–1642), Prime Minister of France who was famous for his patronage of the arts.

Cutwork remained popular and designs were widely available in embroidery magazines up until the 1940s.

## MATERIALS

### Fabrics

It is important to choose a good quality, closely woven linen or cotton fabric, otherwise the cut edges are liable to fray. High thread count linens, 1200–1400 count are ideal. Wash the fabric before using to pre-shrink. Starch and press before transferring the design.

### Threads

There are many threads available that are suitable for cutwork. Traditionally the thread for working the blanket stitch edges and bars would have a matte finish such as broder spécial, floche or Danish flower thread but there is no reason why more lustrous threads, such as silk or fine cotton pearl, cannot be used. Stranded cotton is also suitable.

Fine, needlepoint lace fillings should be worked with linen lace thread. The thread colour should match the fabric as closely as possible.

### Needles

Choose a needle suited to the type of thread that you are using. Ensure that the thread passes through the eye easily and does not untwist. Round threads, such as floche, broder spécial and cotton pearl are easier to thread into a small eyed needle such as a sharp or between. Threads that flatten easily, such as stranded cotton and silk are easier to thread into a large eyed

needle such as a crewel. A fine tapestry needle (size 26–28) is useful for working bars as it is less likely to catch the fabric threads beneath the detached stitches.

### Other

Blanket stitch is easier and faster to work in the hand. Mount the fabric in a frame or hoop when working the bars if maintaining even tension is a concern. Traditionally, the fabric was tacked to parchment to maintain stability while the filling stitches were worked. This allowed the fabric to be held firmly but gave a good amount of flexibility, unlike an embroidery hoop.

Small, fine bladed, sharp embroidery scissors are essential for all forms of cutwork. Blunt blades will result in imprecise edges and a messy finish to the work. Angle the scissors beneath the edge of the blanket stitches when cutting. Cut slowly and carefully. If the embroidery thread is accidentally cut it must be replaced or repaired before the article is laundered.

---

### STITCHES FOR CUTWORK

Blanket stitch
Overcast stitch
Running stitch
Eyelets
    *blanket stitch, pierced, cut, shaded, linked*
Bars
    *blanket stitch, blanket stitch with loop picot*
    *blanket stitch with bullion picot*

*blanket stitch with blanket stitch picot*
*double blanket stitch, needlewoven*
*overcast stitch, 'Y' shaped branch*
*'H' shaped branch*
Laddering
    *overcast stitch 1 and 2, blanket stitch*
Couronnes
    *around cylinder, on fabric, inserting*

# EYELET – BLANKET STITCH

1 Draw a circle on the right side of the fabric to mark the position of the eyelet.

2 Leaving a short tail, work running stitch around the circle.

3 When reaching the first stitch, take the last stitch through it, splitting the stitch.

4 Pull the thread through and bring it to the front just outside the running stitch.

5 Cut the centre of the circle. Alternatively, pierce it with a dressmaker's awl.

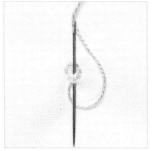

6 With the emerging thread positioned at the bottom, take the needle through the hole and work the first blanket stitch. Ensure the thread is under the tip of the needle.

7 Pull the thread through.

8 Continue working blanket stitches in the same manner, turning the fabric as you work.

9 When the edge is completely covered take the needle to the back just over the loop of the last stitch.

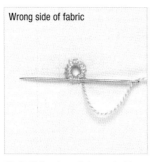

10 Pull the thread through. To secure, take the thread behind the blanket stitches on the back.

11 When working a cut eyelet, trim away the excess fabric on the wrong side.

12 Completed eyelet.

# BLANKET STITCH BAR

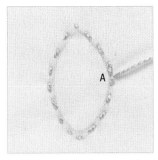

1 Work running stitch around the area to be cut away. Bring the thread to the front just outside the running stitch at the position for the right hand end of the bar (A).

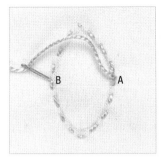

2 Take the needle to the back at B, the position for the left hand end of the bar, and just outside the running stitch.

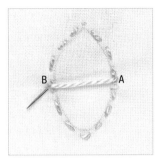

3 Pull the thread through and emerge just below B.

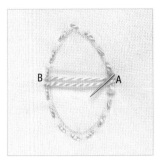

4 Pull the thread through and take the needle to the back just below A. Pull the thread through and emerge just above A.

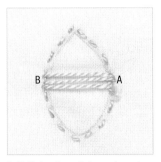

5 Pull the thread through and take the needle to the back just above B. Pull the thread through to complete the foundation bar.

6 Bring the thread to the front just below the left hand end of the lowest foundation stitch.

7 Slide the needle from top to bottom behind the straight stitches. Do not go through the fabric. Position the thread under the tip of the needle.

8 Pull the thread through until the stitch wraps gently around the foundation.

9 Again, slide the needle from top to bottom behind the foundation. Ensure the thread is under the tip of the needle.

10 Pull the thread through. Ensure this stitch lies snugly against the previous stitch without overlapping it.

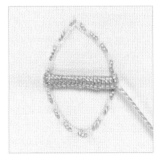

11 Continue working stitches in the same manner until the foundation is completely covered.

12 Take the needle to the back just below the right hand end of the lowest foundation stitch. Pull through and secure on the back.

# DOUBLE BLANKET STITCH BAR

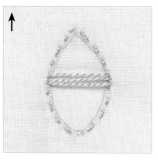

1 Outline the area to be cut away and work the foundation bar following steps 1–5 on page 65.

2 Bring the thread to the front just below the left hand end of the lowest foundation stitch.

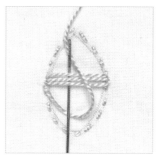

3 Slide the needle behind the straight stitches. Do not go through the fabric. Position the thread under the tip of the needle.

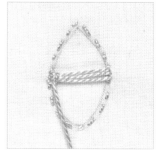

4 Pull the thread through to form a blanket stitch.

5 Continue working blanket stitches across the foundation bar, placing the stitches a thread width apart.

6 After working the last stitch, take the needle to the back of the fabric just below the right hand end of the foundation bar.

7 Pull the thread through. Turn the fabric upside down. Bring the needle to the front just below the left hand end of the foundation bar.

8 Pull the thread through. Slide the needle behind the foundation bar and between the first two blanket stitches. Do not go behind the loops of the previous blanket stitches.

9 Loop the thread from left to right under the tip of the needle.

10 Pull the thread through.

11 Slide the needle behind the foundation bar between the second and third blanket stitches and then loop the thread as before.

12 Pull the thread through. Continue working to the end of the bar, alternating the blanket stitches of the second row with those of the first.

# BLANKET STITCH BAR WITH BLANKET STITCH PICOT

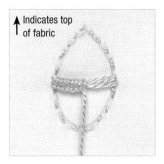

1 Outline the area to be cut away. Work the foundation bar and blanket stitches to the position for the picot following steps 1–11 on page 65.

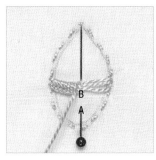

2 Insert a pin into the fabric under the bar at the position for the picot. The length of the picot is A to B.

3 Loop the thread from left to right under the head of the pin and over the bar.

4 Slide the needle behind the bar between the last stitch and the pin. Ensure the loop of thread is under the tip of the needle.

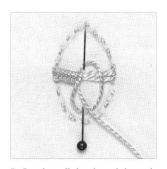

5 Gently pull the thread through.

6 Again loop the thread from left to right under the head of the pin and over the bar.

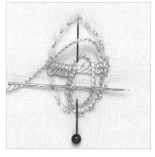

7 Slide the needle, from left to right, behind the first half of the second loop and the second half of the first loop. The second half of the second loop is under the needle tip.

8 Pull the thread through and downwards to form a knot where the pin enters the fabric.

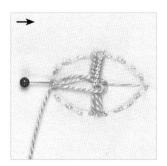

9 Turn the fabric so the pinhead is to your left.

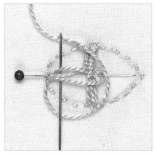

10 Slide the needle behind the three threads. Ensure the thread is under the tip of the needle.

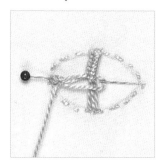

11 Pull the thread through.

12 Work blanket stitches over the threads until you reach the bar. Do not go through the fabric.

## BLANKET STITCH BAR WITH BLANKET STITCH PICOT *CONTINUED*

13 Turn the fabric so the bar is horizontal again.

14 Slide the needle from top to bottom behind the bar. Loop the thread under the needle tip.

15 Pull the thread through. Remove the pin.

16 Continue working blan-ket stitches to the end of the foundation bar. Do not go through the fabric.

# BLANKET STITCH BAR WITH BULLION PICOT

1 Outline the area to be cut. Work the foundation bar and blanket stitch to the picot's position following steps 1–11 on page 65.

2 Take the needle back through the loop of the last worked blanket stitch.

3 Wrap the thread around the tip of the needle in a clockwise direction 5–6 times. Ensure that the wraps lie close together without overlapping.

4 Holding the wraps in place begin to pull the needle through.

5 Pull the thread all the way through. Place your needle inside the loop to separate the wraps from the adjacent thread.

6 Holding the wraps in place, pull the thread to tighten the wraps and curl them into a loop.

7 Slide the needle behind the bar and just to the right of the bullion loop. Ensure the thread is under the tip of the needle.

8 Pull the thread through and continue working blanket stitches to the end of the foundation bar.

# BLANKET STITCH BAR WITH LOOPED PICOT

1 Outline the area to be cut. Work the foundation bar and blanket stitch to the picot's position following steps 1–11 on page 65.

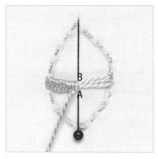

2 Insert a pin into the fabric as shown. The length of the picot is A to B.

3 Take the thread from left to right behind the head of the pin.

4 On the right hand side of the pin, slide the needle from top to bottom behind the foundation bar.

5 Pull the thread through.

6 Loop the thread as shown. Slide the needle from left to right behind the picot, under the left half of the loop and over the right half.

7 Pull the thread through, pulling firmly to the right to hold the loop around the pin.

8 Remove the pin. Continue working blanket stitches to the end of the foundation bar.

# NEEDLEWOVEN BAR

1 Outline the area to be cut and work a foundation bar with four threads.

2 Bring the thread to the front just below the left hand end of the lowest foundation stitch.

3 Slide the needle under the two upper foundation threads. Do not go through the fabric.

4 Pull the thread through.

## NEEDLEWOVEN BAR *CONTINUED*

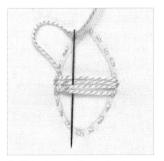

5 Slide the needle under the two lower foundation threads. Do not go through the fabric.

6 Pull the thread through.

7 Keeping the stitches close together, repeat steps 3–6 across the bar. Take the needle to the back next to the right hand end of the nearest foundation stitch.

8 Pull the thread through.

## OVERCAST BAR

1 Outline the area to be cut away and work the bar following steps 1–5 on page 65.

2 Bring the thread to the front just below the left hand end of the lowest foundation stitch.

3 Slide the needle from top to bottom behind the foundation bar. Do not go through the fabric.

4 Pull the thread through until it wraps firmly around the foundation bar.

5 Again take the needle behind the bar in the same manner as before.

6 Pull the thread through as before, ensuring the wrap lies snugly alongside the previous wrap.

7 Continue in the same manner along the bar. Take the needle to the back below the right hand end of the lowest foundation stitch.

8 Pull the thread through.

# BRANCHED BAR – Y SHAPE

**1** Outline the area to be cut away and work the first foundation bar following steps 1–5 on page 65. This bar forms the right branch and trunk of the Y.

**2** Following steps 6–11 on page 65, work close blanket stitches along the bar until reaching the position for the left branch (A). Keep the purl edge towards the second branch.

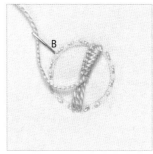

**3** Take the needle to the back at B, the opposite end of the left branch.

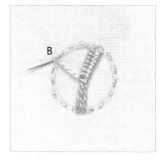

**4** Pull the thread through and emerge just below B.

**5** Pull the thread through. Take the needle through the purl of the last blanket stitch.

**6** Pull the thread through and take the needle to the back below the left hand end of the previous stitch.

**7** Pull the thread through to complete the foundation bar.

**8** Bring the thread to the front just below the left hand end of the lowest foundation stitch.

**9** Work blanket stitch along the bar until it is completely covered.

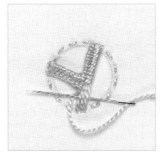

**10** Slide the needle from right to left behind the trunk of the Y. Ensure the thread is under the tip of the needle.

**11** Pull the thread through.

**12** Continue working blanket stitches to the end of the trunk.

# BRANCHED BAR – H SHAPE

1 Outline the area to be cut away and work a foundation bar following steps 1–5 on page 65. This bar forms the right hand side of the H.

2 Following steps 6–11 on page 65, work close blanket stitches along the bar. Keep the purl edge towards the inside of the H.

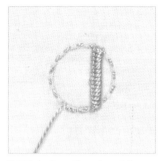

3 Stitch along the edge of the shape to the position for the left hand side of the H.

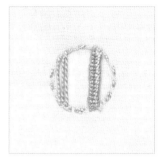

4 Work a second foundation bar in the same manner as the first bar.

5 Work close blanket stitches until approximately halfway along the bar. Keep the purl edge towards the inside of the H.

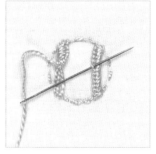

6 Take the needle through the purl of the middle blanket stitch on the first bar.

7 Pull the thread through. Take the needle through the purl of the last blanket stitch on the second bar.

8 Pull the thread through and take the needle through the same purl on the first bar as before.

9 Pull the thread through to complete the foundation bar.

10 Work close blanket stitches across this bar until it is completely covered, keeping the purl edge towards the base of the H.

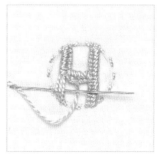

11 Slide the needle behind the vertical bar and below the previous bar. Ensure the thread is under the tip of the needle.

12 Continue working blanket stitches to the base of the bar.

# LADDERING WITH BLANKET STITCH

↑ indicates top of fabric

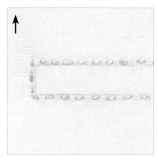

1 Work two parallel rows of running stitch. Work the ends in running stitch.

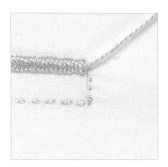

2 Following the instructions on page 32, work close blanket stitch, from left to right, along the upper edge. Ensure the purl is placed along the edge to be cut.

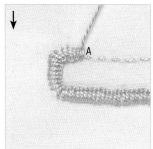

3 Turning the fabric, work blanket stitch along the right hand end and then along the lower edge to the position for the first bar (A).

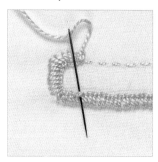

4 Take the needle through the purl of the blanket stitch directly opposite. Do not go through the fabric.

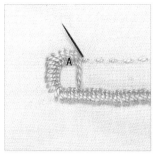

5 Take the needle to the back just to the left of A. Pull the thread through and emerge just to the right.

6 Pull the thread through. Again, take the needle through the purl of the same blanket stitch on the opposite side.

7 Pull the thread through to complete the foundation bar. Work blanket stitching across the foundation bar following the instructions on page 65.

8 Work blanket stitch to the position of the next bar and work in the same manner as the first bar.

9 Continue in the same manner to the end of the running stitches, finishing at the starting position.

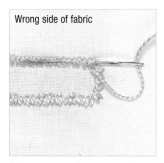

10 To secure, take the needle to the back. Take it through the stitches on the back and pull through.

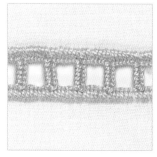

11 Cut away the fabric from behind the bars, following the instructions on page 76.

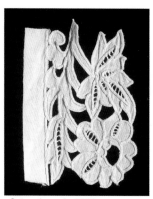

*Cutwork, early 1900s*

73

# WORKING A COURONNE (RING) AROUND A CYLINDER

1 Thread a long length of thread into a needle. Wrap it 2–3 times around a cylinder of the desired diameter, eg a knitting needle or pencil.

2 Holding the wraps in place, take the needle behind the wraps. Ensure the thread is under the tip of the needle.

3 Pull the thread through until it is firm around the wrapped threads.

4 Again take the needle behind the wrapped threads. Ensure the thread is under the tip of the needle.

5 Pull the thread through until it is firm around the wrapped threads.

6 Move the ring onto a slightly thinner cylinder to make it easier to work the stitches.

7 Continue working detached blanket stitches around the wrapped threads in the same manner until the ring is tightly packed with stitches.

8 Either secure the thread in the back of the blanket stitches or continue working rounds of detached stitches.

# WORKING A COURONNE ON FABRIC

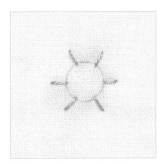

1 Draw a circle on the fabric. Work 4–6 straight stitches out from the circle ensuring they are evenly spaced.

2 Using a new thread, take it behind the stitches around the circle. Do not go through the fabric.

3 Repeat 1–2 more times. Again, do not go through the fabric.

4 Using the same thread, take the needle behind the circle of threads. Ensure the thread is under the tip of the needle.

## WORKING A COURONNE ON FABRIC *CONTINUED*

5 Pull the thread through until it is firm around the circle of threads.

6 Again take the needle behind the circle of threads. Ensure the thread is under the tip of the needle.

7 Pull the thread through until it is firm. Continue working in the same manner until the circle is tightly packed with stitches.

8 Cut the straight stitches and remove the couronne.

# INSERTING A COURONNE

1 Position the couronne on the fabric and pin in place as shown.

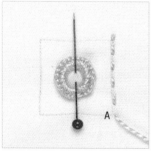

2 Work running stitch around the shape to be cut out, up to where the first bar will be positioned (A).

3 Take the needle through the purl of the blanket stitch that aligns with the bar. Do not go through the fabric.

4 Pull the thread through. Take the needle to the back just to the left of A. Pull the thread through and emerge just to the right of A.

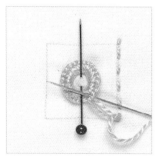

5 Take the needle through the purl of the same blanket stitch.

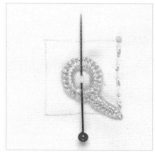

6 Pull the thread through to complete the foundation bar. Work blanket stitch across the foundation following the instructions on page 65.

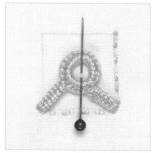

7 Work running stitch to the position of the next bar and work this bar in the same manner as the first.

8 Continue in the same manner until all bars are worked and the couronne is secured in place. Remove the pin.

# CUTWORK – ORDER OF WORK AND CUTTING OUT

1 Work running stitch around all areas to be worked with blanket stitch. When reaching the position of the first bar, take the needle over the area to be cut away.

2 Work the foundation bar following steps 1–5 on page 65.

3 Work blanket stitch back across the foundation bar until it is completely covered. Do not take the stitches through the fabric.

4 Continue working running stitch to the position of the next bar and repeat steps 2–3.

5 Continue in this manner until all bars are complete and running stitch has been worked along all lines to be blanket stitched.

6 Work blanket stitch along the design lines covering the running stitch and ends of the bars. Ensure the purls of the blanket stitches face the edges to be cut.

7 Using small, sharp scissors, pierce one area to be cut away from the right side of the fabric.

8 Cut along the centre of the shape, carefully lifting the bars with the scissors.

9 Turn to the wrong side. Holding the scissors flat and against the blanket stitched edges, cut away the fabric very carefully.

10 Trim all loose threads.

11 Press the embroidery from the wrong side.

12 Completed cutwork.

# Hedebo embroidery

## Also known as Danish work, Hebeo, Danish cut work

Hedebo embroidery is unusual in that there are three distinct forms that all fall under the same name but use quite different techniques. It is the third and most recent form that we will explore here. Originating in Denmark, Hedebo gets its name from the flat tract of land known as 'Heden' (the heath) that lies between Copenhagen and Roskilde, the former capital. This form of embroidery was little known outside Denmark until almost the end of the 19th century, as it was intended solely for the use of the embroiderer and her family. It was traditionally used on the cuffs, collars and shoulder pieces of men's and women's shirts, decorative pieces that were used on festive occasions, bedspreads, pillowcases and sheets. In Denmark, a bedspread was laid over a bright red lining to emphasise the design.

When a baby was born, the women of the family and female servants would begin to prepare a trousseau that was lavishly ornamented with beautiful embroidery. The fabric was spun and woven, then embroidered in the household.

### HISTORY

The oldest form of this embroidery dates back to the 16th century and used designs that were adapted from traditional wood carvings. Robust surface embroidery, largely in chain stitch, was combined with drawn thread fillings and mainly conventional floral motifs were stitched.

The second form of Hedebo evolved around 1840 and whilst it retained the floral motifs worked in satin stitch, the amount of cut and drawn spaces was increased, giving the work a more geometric and formal appearance, similar to Italian reticella embroidery.

The final evolution saw Hedebo become popular in other parts of the world. The geometric nature of the cut shapes disappeared and very little surface stitchery remained. These changes gave the work a very distinctive look that set it apart from other forms of cut work.

The cut shapes are edged with Hedebo stitch, a form of buttonhole that is characteristic of this work, and filled with needlelace stitches. Unlike most forms of cutwork embroidery, the edges of the shapes are outlined with running stitch, cut and turned under before the Hedebo stitch is worked to secure them. Couronnes or rings are also characteristic of this work and are made on a Hedebo ring stick, a tool about 18cm (7") long that is graduated in steps of several diameters, enabling different sized rings to be made.

Although the last form of Hedebo embroidery is regarded by some as inferior, at its finest it is exceedingly beautiful and intricate work.

> "Much of the work is akin to lace and its very high standard of technique equals Ayrshire work, its British contemporary."
>
> *Barbara Snook 'Learning to Embroider'*

*Hedebo upper shirt sleeve, prior to 1840*

## MATERIALS

### Fabrics

Traditionally, the embroidery was worked on natural linen with a two stranded linen thread that was slightly darker than the fabric. The passion for whitework led to both the fabric and the thread being bleached and worked, white on white.

Hedebo is worked on closely woven even weave linen or cotton fabric that does not fray easily when cut.

### Threads

The needlelace fillings should be worked with a linen lace thread as cotton is not strong enough and will fluff and break. A length sufficient to complete the filling should be used to prevent joins. Surface embroidery is worked in a softer cotton thread such as broder spécial, floche or stranded cotton.

### Needles

Surface embroidery is worked with a sharp or crewel needle of a size suited to the thread. Needlelace fillings can be worked with a fine tapestry needle to prevent accidentally splitting the threads.

### Other

Mount the fabric in a hoop or frame. Sharp, fine pointed embroidery scissors are essential to cut away unwanted fabric from the shapes.

*Hedebo upper shirt sleeve, prior to 1840*

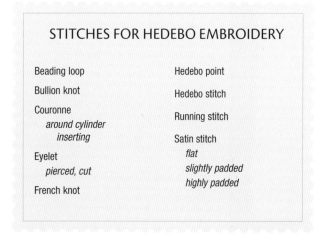

## STITCHES FOR HEDEBO EMBROIDERY

| | |
|---|---|
| Beading loop | Hedebo point |
| Bullion knot | Hedebo stitch |
| Couronne<br>    *around cylinder*<br>    *inserting* | Running stitch |
| | Satin stitch<br>    *flat* |
| Eyelet<br>    *pierced, cut* | *slightly padded*<br>*highly padded* |
| French knot | |

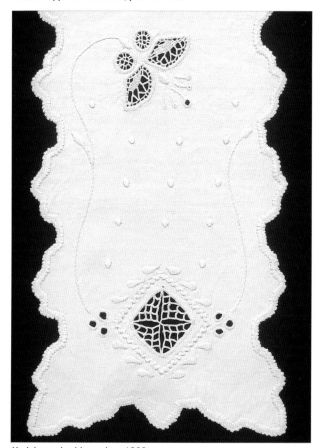

*Hedebo embroidery, circa 1860*

# BEADING LOOP

*Beading loop is used to create a row of open stitches. It is worked into a base of Hedebo stitch.*

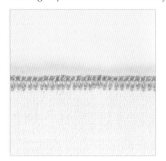

1 Begin with a row of Hedebo stitch following the instructions on page 81.

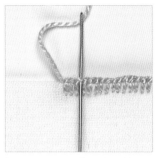

2 Secure a new thread and bring to the front. Take a stitch through the loop of the base row.

3 Tighten the thread until a loop remains.

4 Take the needle, from back to front, through the loop and pull through.

5 Repeat along the length of the Hedebo stitch, making loops with the desired spacing.

6 Continue for the required distance.

*Modern Hedebo collar, circa 1905*

# HEDEBO POINT

*Work a base of Hedebo stitch (see page 81). These points can be made with any number of stitches. This example is worked on a base of six stitches and decreases one stitch in every row. All rows are worked left to right.*

1 Bring the thread to the front through the loop at the top of the existing stitches.

2 Whip the top loop of the six Hedebo stitches to the left of the starting point.

3 Stitching through the whipped loops, work five Hedebo stitches.

4 Whip back along the five top loops.

5 Stitching through the whipped loops, work four Hedebo stitches.

6 Whip back along the four top loops.

7 Stitching through the whipped loops, work three Hedebo stitches.

8 Whip back along the three top loops.

9 Stitching through the whipped loops, work two Hedebo stitches.

10 Whip back along the two top loops.

11 Stitching through the whipped loop, work one Hedebo stitch.

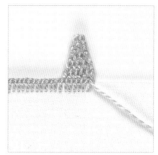

12 Return the thread to the base of the point by whipping down the right side.

# HEDEBO STITCH

*The edge of the fabric is cut and folded under before commencing the stitch.*

1 Secure the thread and bring to the surface in the fold of the fabric.

2 Take a stitch through the fabric and pull through until a small loop remains.

3 Take the needle, from back to front through the loop.

4 Pull the thread up until the loop sits firmly.

5 Take a second stitch and pull through until a small loop remains.

6 Take the needle from back to front through the loop and pull the thread up until the loop sits firmly.

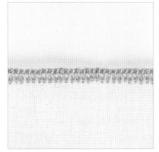

7 Continue working in this manner.

*Modern Hedebo mats, after 1880*

*Old Hedebo shirt cuffs, prior to 1840*

# Madeira embroidery

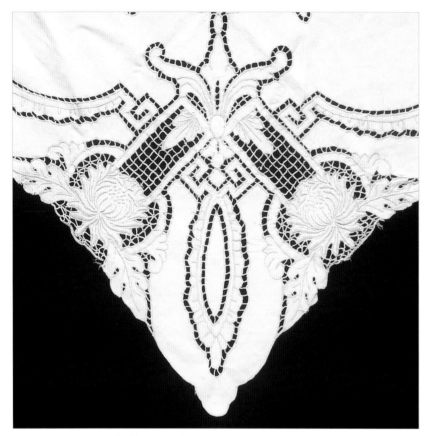

*Madeira work, corner of tablecloth, early 1900s*

"…white embroidery by hand is done only in limited quantities by skilled professionals in places such as Hong Kong, Madeira and Venice."

*Erica Wilson, Erica Wilson's Embroidery Book*

Madeira embroidery encompasses a wide range of styles including cutwork and broderie anglaise. Its uniqueness lies in the origins of the work as, like Ayrshire and Mountmellick embroidery, it stems from an organised embroidery trade, designed to provide viable work for women. Unlike Ayrshire and Mountmellick, the embroidery of Madeira is still produced for sale today.

The Madeira Islands are part of Portugal and consist of four land masses – Madeira, Porto Santo, Desertas and Selvagens – that lie approximately 800kms off the west coast of Africa. Madeira is the largest of the four islands. Embroidery has always been part of the island's cultural history but it has only been through the intervention of the English, Germans and Americans that Madeira work has become known around the world and prized for its fineness and the artistry of its designs.

## HISTORY

The Madeira Islands are blessed with a tropical climate and they were a popular holiday destination in the 1800s for Europeans from colder climates. During the 1850s, Elizabeth Phelps, the daughter of a wine merchant, noticed that the women on Madeira were very proficient with a needle and thread and she asked that they stitch some pieces that she sent home to England. She introduced the techniques of broderie anglaise and from this, a cottage industry grew. German entrepreneurs saw the potential of high quality embroidered goods and broadened the industry to cater to the needs of the world market. By the 1880s this style of embroidery was known as 'broderie Madère' or 'Madeira work'. By 1900 the industry employed thousands of workers and continued happily until the outbreak of World War 1 when Portugal joined the Allies. All Germans living on the islands were interned and their business interests confiscated. This brought the embroidery industry to a standstill until local and foreign companies saw a chance to enter an already established market. An influx of Syrians began to dominate the trade but their decision to manufacture in large volume and flood the world market led to a decline in the quality of the materials used and discredited the reputation of Madeira work. During the period 1916–1925, the industry suffered a serious decline.

In 1925 the Imperial Linen Company was established by Leo Behrens and Charles Rolland, two enterprising businessmen who recognised that it was the lack of change in the embroidery style, rather than diminishing craftsmanship that had led to the decline in sales. Charles Rolland travelled to Europe and sourced new fabrics and techniques, appliqué and coloured threads from France, organdie from Switzerland, shadow work from Italy and cutwork from Spain. The Imperial Linen Company adopted these techniques and developed them into the style that is now known as Madeira embroidery.

Embroidery in Madeira is still a cottage industry. Designs are applied to the fabric in the factory, then collected by an agent who distributes the work to the embroiderers. Women work at home on the pieces which are returned to the factory for finishing. Because the stitching is done in the home, the stitches and techniques are passed down through the generations and a young child will learn to stitch at her mother's or grandmother's knee. When she becomes proficient, the young embroiderer will be registered and supplied with work by an agent.

In the 1920s the Embroidery Guild (GREMIO) was founded to establish wages and benefits, and to set standards for the industry. Pieces to be sold have to pass inspection and were marked with a small silver tag that has recently been replaced with a paper tag. This tag guarantees that the embroidery has met the most stringent quality standards.

## MATERIALS

### Fabrics

Fine, closely woven linen and translucent organdie are the most commonly used fabrics and they are often used together in the magnificent appliqué pieces that are synonymous with Madeira embroidery. Silk chiffon and cotton batiste are used for clothing.

### Threads

Floche is the most commonly used thread for Madeira embroidery. It is a five ply non-divisible thread with a soft twist that was, at one time, manufactured in seven weights, 40 being the finest. 16 is the size that is now most commonly available. Broder spécial is also suitable.

### Needles

The embroiderers on Madeira use a size 7 between almost exclusively for their work. A between is a very short needle with a small, round eye. A sharp is similar but has a longer shaft if you find a between difficult to handle.

### Other

All Madeira embroidery is worked in the hand. Hoops and frames are not used but each embroiderer employs a plastic finger shield over the index finger to protect from needle stabs while allowing speed and control. The fabric is stretched over the shield and should be positioned so that the embroiderer always stitches towards the body.

| STITCHES FOR MADEIRA EMBROIDERY | | |
|---|---|---|
| Blanket stitch | Granitos | Seed stitch |
| *padded* | Long and short stitch | Shadow work |
| *scallops* | Outline stitch | *closed herringbone* |
| Back stitch | Pin stitch | Stem stitch |
| Eyelet | Satin stitch | |
| *linked* | *flat* | |
| *Madeira flower* | *slightly padded* | |
| *pierced* | *highly padded* | |

# EYELET – MADEIRA FLOWER

**1** Mark the centre of the flower with a small circle and each of the six petals with a line.

**2** Work an eyelet for the centre, following steps 1–9 on page 35.

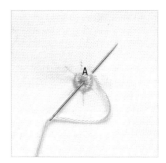

**3** Take the needle to the back through the hole and emerge at the base of a petal (A).

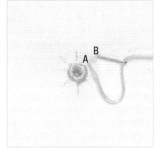

**4** Pull the thread through and take the needle to the back at B, the tip of the petal.

**5** Pull the thread through and emerge at A again.

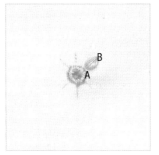

**6** Pull the thread through. Continue working straight stitches from A–B until the petal is the desired thickness.

**7** Take the needle to the back at B and emerge at the base of the next petal marking.

**8** Work this petal and all remaining petals in the same manner.

# GRANITOS

*Work these satin dots over the curve of your index finger to obtain the best result.*

**1** Secure the thread on the back of the fabric and bring it to the front at A.

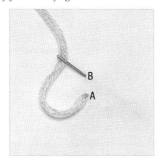

**2** Take the needle to the back at B.

**3** Pull the thread through. Emerge at A, taking care to come through exactly the same hole in the fabric as before.

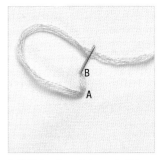

**4** Pull the thread through. Take the needle to the back at B through exactly the same hole in the fabric as before.

# GRANITOS *CONTINUED*

   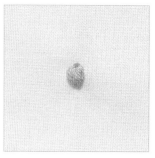

5 Loop the thread to the left of the first stitch and begin to gently pull the thread through.

6 Pull until the stitch lies alongside the first stitch.

7 Work a third stitch, looping the thread to the right of the first stitch.

8 Gently pull the thread through. Work the required number of stitches in the same manner, always alternating from side to side. Secure the thread on the back.

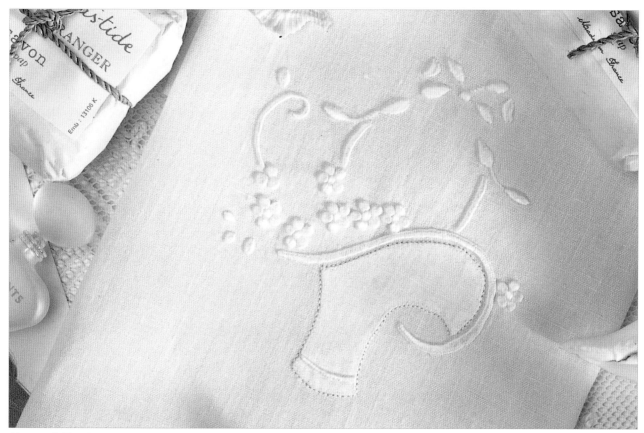

*Moments in Time by Lillie McAnge*

# LONG AND SHORT STITCH

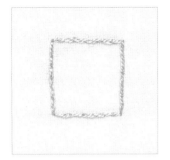

1 Draw the shape to be filled on the fabric. Outline the shape in split stitch.

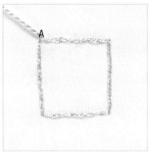

2 **First row** Secure a new thread on the back of the fabric and bring it to the front at A, just outside the outline.

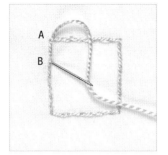

3 Take the needle to the back at B, inside the shape.

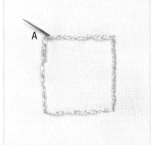

4 Pull the thread through. Emerge just beyond the outline, very close to A.

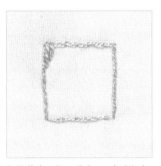

5 Pull the thread through. Work a second stitch that is slightly shorter than the first stitch and parallel to it.

6 Continue working parallel stitches very close together. Alternate between long and short stitches.

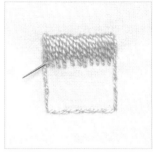

7 **Second row** Bring the thread to the front, splitting the first stitch of the previous row. All subsequent rows are worked with stitches of the same length.

8 Pull the thread through. Begin the next row.

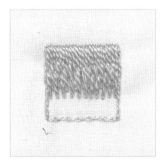

9 Continue across the row, emerging through a stitch of the previous row each time.

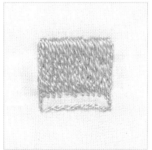

10 **Subsequent rows** Continue working rows in the same manner until your shape is almost filled.

11 For the last row, work long and short stitches, taking the stitches just over the split stitch outline.

12 Secure the thread on the back.

# PIN STITCH

*Pin stitch is the basic stitch used for Madeira appliqué.*

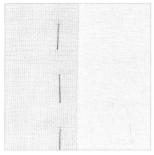

1 Turn under the raw edge on the appliqué piece and finger press. Tack the piece to the right side of the base fabric.

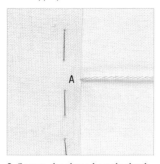

2 Secure the thread on the back of the fabric and bring it to the front at A.

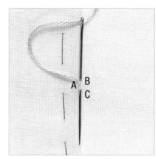

3 Take the needle from B to C through the base fabric only. B is directly in line with A.

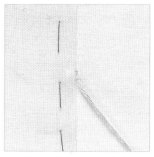

4 Pull the thread through firmly to draw the fabric threads together. A small hole will form at each end of the stitch.

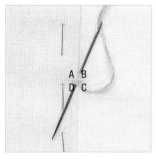

5 Take the needle to the back at B and emerge at D through both fabrics. D is directly below A and to the left of C.

6 Pull the thread through.

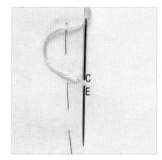

7 Take the needle from C to E through the base fabric only.

8 Pull the thread through firmly to draw the fabric threads together.

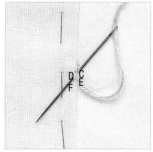

9 Take the needle to the back at C and emerge at F through both fabrics. F is directly below D and to the left of E.

10 Pull the thread through. Continue working stitches in the same manner.

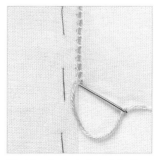

11 After the last stitch, take the needle to the back through the last hole in the base fabric.

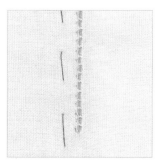

12 Pull the thread through and secure on the back.

# SHADOW WORK – CLOSED HERRINGBONE STITCH

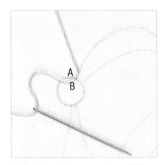

1 Begin with a waste knot. Take the thread to the back at A. Bring the thread to the front at B, at the end of the shape.

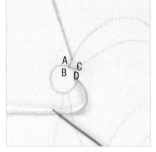

2 Take the thread to the back at C. Bring the thread to the front at D.

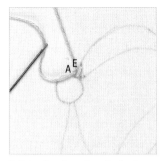

3 Take the thread to the back at E. Bring the thread to the front at A.

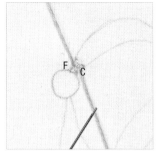

4 Take the thread to the back at F. Bring the thread to the front at C.

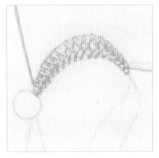

5 Continue working from side to side until the shape is full.

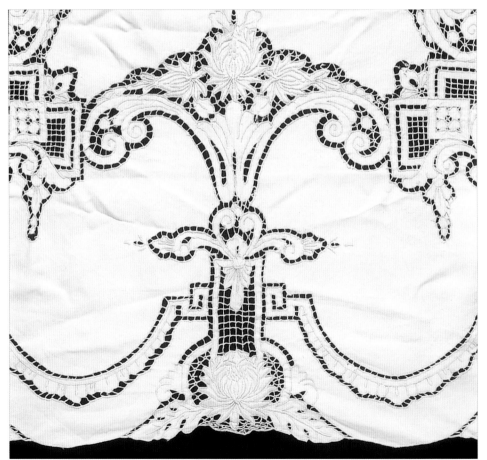

*Madeira work, side of tablecloth, early 1900s*

# Mountmellick embroidery

## Also known as Mellick work, Irish white embroidery, Mountmellick lace

Mountmellick embroidery originated in Ireland and is named for the town of Mountmellick in County Laois.

This style of stitching is highly textured, having a boldness and coarseness that sets it apart from other white on white embroidery. It relies purely on heavy surface embroidery with as little thread as possible passing across the back of the fabric.

The impact of the stitching owes much to the thick, matte cotton thread that is used, contrasting with the smooth lustrous surface of the satin jean that is the traditional ground fabric.

Most Mountmellick work was done for use in the household – tablecloths, coverlets, cushion covers and pillow shams – and also embellished christening gowns.

Floral designs predominate and were originally inspired by the plants that grow along the Owenass River that runs through the town of Mountmellick, such as blackberries, dog rose, ivy, oak, barley, woodbine and wild clematis. Cultivated plants such as passion flower, cyclamen, tiger lily and daffodils were also frequently used in designs. Commemorative pieces often use other symbols such as the harp and shamrocks. Heavy knitted fringing is often used to edge articles.

*Doiley, circa 1880*

"Mountmellick embroidery is handsome, strong and durable work usually executed with Strutt's Knitting Cotton, in sizes varying from No. 6 to No. 14, on a ground of white satin jean; the embroidery is much raised, and is consequently thick and heavy…
It is rich and effective in appearance, not difficult of execution when once the stitches are mastered."

*Weldon's Practical – Mountmellick Embroidery (first series)*

# HISTORY

In 1657 the Society of Friends (Quakers) settled in Mountmellick and helped the small village to grow into a town of eight thousand people with a large manufacturing industry. This included tanneries, breweries, cotton and woollen mills. Mountmellick became known as the Manchester of Ireland.

Embroidery has a long association with the Quakers who fostered the tradition by teaching it and adapting it to their own designs. A Quaker school was opened in Mountmellick in 1786. Girls at this school were instructed in embroidery as a way to earn money for their books. The style of stitching now known as Mountmellick was introduced around 1825 by Johanna Carter.

Her work was displayed at the Irish Industrial Exhibition of 1853, where she was referred to as a designer and manufacturer of embroidered quilts, toilet covers and doyleys.

Little is known about Johanna Carter. It is thought that she may have been a Quaker but an educational report of 1824 lists her as a member of the Church of Ireland. Sadly, the town's prosperity was not to last and the Potato Famine of 1845 saw Ireland's population halve and extreme hardship befell almost everyone. To help relieve the financial distress of poor families the women worked in the production of embroidered household goods, particularly bedspreads that were then sold. This brought the embroidery to the attention of a much wider audience and by 1850 it was enormously popular throughout Britain. Working the coarse stitches

was far less taxing than fine techniques such as Ayrshire and broderie anglaise so Mountmellick became a popular pastime for middle class ladies during the Victorian era. Its popularity was enhanced when Weldon published eight volumes about this style of embroidery.

In 1880, a Mrs Millner started the Industrial Association in Mountmellick. Her aim was 'to provide a livelihood for distressed Irish gentlewomen'. She

was able to employ fifty women to embroider for her.

Irish emigrants took their unique style of embroidery with them when they left their homes for new countries such as America, Canada and Australia.

As with most hand embroidery techniques, Mountmellick fell out of favour in the early part of the 20th century, however during the early 1970s, Sister Teresa McCarthy of the

*Mountmellick style embroidery*

Presentation Convent in Mountmellick began a revival of this form of embroidery. She set about collecting traditional pieces, researching the stitches and eventually began teaching them to others. This work still continues today.

Mountmellick embroidery is considered to be unique in that it is the only form of embroidery from the 19th century that can claim to be entirely Irish in origin and design.

## MATERIALS

### Fabrics

The traditional fabric for Mountmellick work is known as satin jean. It is a tightly woven, medium to heavyweight 100% cotton fabric with a soft lustrous surface. Authentic satin jean is still available today from specialist suppliers. As an alternative, look in the furnishing fabric department for plain cotton sateen that is manufactured for curtains and upholstery.

Always launder your fabric before using to pre-shrink it. It is also advisable to machine zigzag the edges to prevent them from fraying.

### Threads

Matte, unmercerised cotton threads that contrasted with the satin fabric were traditionally used. Various thicknesses were utilised, but generally the same thickness was used throughout one piece. Thread is now available that is manufactured specifically for Mountmellick embroidery and is made in three sizes – no. 2, no. 3 and no. 4. Alternatively, knitting and crochet cottons can be used but choose those that are matte

and unmercerised. Many of these threads are now mercerised, giving them a lustrous finish rather than the matte that is authentic.

### Needles

As the thread for Mountmellick embroidery is thick, choose a chenille or crewel needle to suit the thread. Both of these needle types have long, large eyes and are easy to thread. Long darners and yarn darners are suitable for working bullion knots.

The knitted fringes that are such a feature of this form of embroidery are generally worked with 2.75–3.25mm knitting needles (English sizes 12–10; US sizes 2–3).

### Other

Mount your fabric in an embroidery hoop or frame to help maintain even stitch tension and to prevent the fabric from puckering. Work bullion knots in the hand as they are much easier when you are able to manipulate the fabric.

| STITCHES FOR MOUNTMELLICK WORK | |
|---|---|
| Back stitch | Fern stitch |
| Blanket stitch | Fishbone stitch |
| crossed | Flake stitch |
| detached | French knot |
| edging | Fly stitch |
| indented | Gordian knot stitch |
| in the opposite direction | Herringbone stitch |
| knotted | Honeycomb stitch |
| long and short | Knitted fringe |
| padded | Loop stitch |
| partial pinwheel | Mountmellick stitch |
| pinwheel | Outline stitch |
| saw tooth | Overcast stitch |
| up and down | indented |
| Braid stitch | Palestrina stitch |
| Brick stitch | Point de reprise stitch |
| Bullion knot | |
| Cable stitch | Portuguese knotted stem stitch |
| Cable chain stitch | Running stitch |
| Cable plait stitch | Satin stitch |
| Chain stitch | flat |
| rosette, twisted | slightly padded |
| whipped | highly padded |
| Coral stitch | Scroll stitch |
| single | Seed stitch |
| zigzag | Spider web |
| Cording stitch | whipped |
| Couching | Split stitch |
| Bokhara | Stem stitch |
| Roumanian | whipped |
| Cretan stitch | Thorn stitch |
| Detached chain | Trailing stitch |
| Feather stitch | Trellis stitch |
| single | Van Dyke stitch |
| double | Wave stitch |
| closed | Wheatear stitch |
| Spanish knotted | |

# BLANKET STITCH – CROSSED

1 Secure the thread on the back of the fabric and bring it to the front at A.

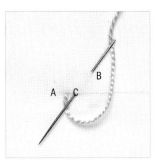

2 Take the needle to the back at B and emerge at C, ensuring it is angled as shown. Ensure the thread is under the tip of the needle.

3 Pull the thread through until it lies snugly against the emerging thread but does not distort the fabric.

4 Take the needle to the back at D and emerge at E, ensuring it is angled as shown. Ensure the thread lies under the tip of the needle.

5 Pull the thread through as before. This stitch will cross the previous stitch.

6 Continue working stitches in the same manner.

7 To finish, take the needle to the back of the fabric just over the last loop.

8 Pull the thread through and secure on the back.

## Opus Teutonicum

Some of the earliest pieces of whitework that still exist today date back to the 12th century. They are mainly embroidered cloths that were used as altar coverings particularly during the period of Lent. Because of their German origins, these embroideries were often referred to in church records as Opus Teutonicum.

By the 14th century, similar altar cloths were found in the churches of Germany's neighbours. The beauty of whitework had spread to Scandinavia and Northern Italy.

# BLANKET STITCH – DETACHED

1  Secure the thread on the back of the fabric and bring it to the front at A. Take the thread to the back the required distance away, forming a straight stitch.

2  Bring the thread to the front at A.

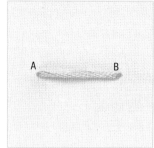

3  Take it to the back at B to complete the foundation for the blanket stitches.

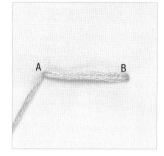

4  Bring the needle to the front just below A. Pull the thread through.

5  Slide the needle behind the straight stitches. Do not go through the fabric. Ensure the thread is under the tip of the needle.

6  Pull the thread through until the stitch wraps snugly around the foundation.

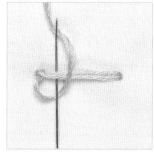

7  Again, slide the needle from top to bottom behind the foundation. Ensure the thread is under the tip of the needle.

8  Pull the thread through. Ensure this stitch lies snugly against the previous stitch without overlapping it.

9  Continue working stitches in the same manner until the foundation is completely covered.

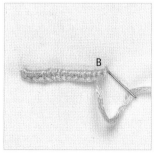

10  Take the needle to the back of the fabric just below B.

11  Pull the thread through and secure on the back.

# BLANKET STITCH – EDGING

*Mountmellick embroideries are edged prior to attaching a knitted fringe.*

1 Secure the thread on the back of the fabric and bring it to the front at A.

2 Take the needle to the back at A again and emerge beyond the edge of the fabric. Ensure the thread is under the tip of the needle.

3 Pull the thread through until the loop lies against the emerging thread but does not distort the fabric.

4 Take the needle to the back at B and emerge beyond the edge of the fabric. Ensure the thread lies under the tip of the needle.

5 Pull the thread through as before.

6 Continue working stitches in the same manner.

7 After working the last stitch, take the needle to the back of the fabric just over the first loop.

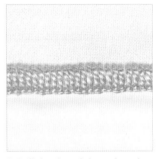

8 Pull the thread through and secure on the back.

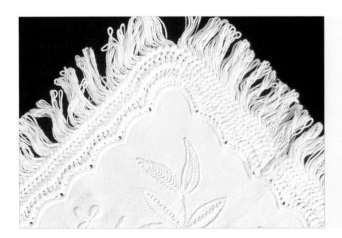

## Mountmellick work

Between 1890 and 1898, Weldon Publishers of London published four volumes called 'Weldon's Practical Mountmellick Embroidery'.

Altogether, they published eight books on Mountmellick work, making it extremely popular.

# BLANKET STITCH – INDENTED

1 Secure the thread on the back of the fabric and bring it to the front at A.

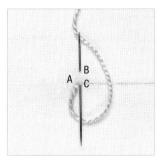

2 Take the needle to the back at B and emerge at C. Ensure the thread is under the tip of the needle.

3 Pull the thread through until it lies snugly against the emerging thread but does not distort the fabric.

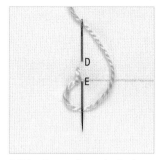

4 Take the needle to the back at D and emerge at E. Ensure the thread is under the tip of the needle.

5 Pull the thread through as before to work a second stitch slightly longer than the first.

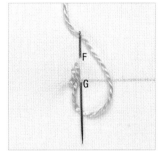

6 Take the needle to the back at F and emerge at G. Ensure the thread lies under the tip of the needle.

7 Pull the thread through as before to work a third stitch slightly longer than the second.

8 Work a fourth stitch in the same manner, making it slightly longer than the previous stitch.

9 Work a stitch the same length as the third stitch, followed by a stitch the same as the second and then another the same as the first.

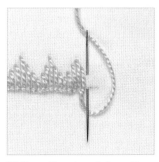

10 Repeating steps 4–9, continue working stitches across the row.

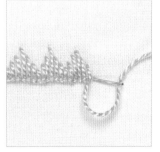

11 To finish, take the needle to the back of the fabric just over the last loop.

12 Pull the thread through and secure on the back.

# BLANKET STITCH – IN THE OPPOSITE DIRECTION (RIGHT TO LEFT)

*It is sometimes helpful to work blanket stitch from right to left, and fortunately it is a stitch that readily allows you to do this.*

1 Secure the thread on the back of the fabric and bring it to the front at A, on the right hand side.

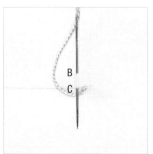

2 Take the needle to the back at B and emerge at C. Ensure the thread is under the tip of the needle.

3 Pull the thread through until it lies snugly against the emerging thread but does not distort the fabric.

4 Take the needle to the back at D and emerge at E. Ensure the thread lies under the tip of the needle.

5 Pull the thread through as before.

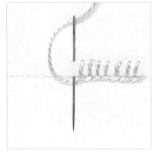

6 Continue working stitches in the same manner.

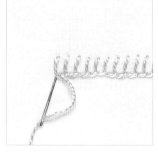

7 To finish, take the needle to the back of the fabric just over the last loop.

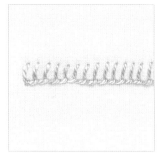

8 Pull the thread through and secure on the back.

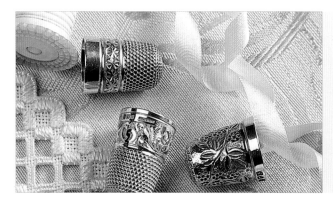

## Indian muslins

India's tradition of weaving fine muslins dates back to the 4th century. These diaphanous fabrics were often bleached with diluted lemon juice and starched with rice water. They were given such romantic names as 'woven wind', 'scorched tears' and 'dew of light'.

# BLANKET STITCH – KNOTTED

1 Secure the thread on the back of the fabric and bring it to the front at A, on the lower left hand side.

2 Wrap the thread once around your left thumb in a clockwise direction.

3 Slide the needle through the loop of thread.

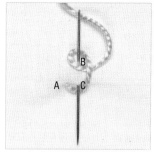

4 Keeping the loop on the needle, take the needle from B–C. Ensure the emerging thread is under the tip of the needle.

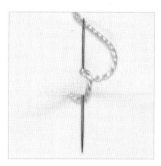

5 Pull the thread firmly so the emerging thread is taut and the loop tightens around the needle.

6 Keeping your thumb over the loop pull the needle and thread through to complete the first stitch.

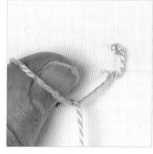

7 Wrap the thread around your thumb in the same manner as before.

8 Again, slide the needle through the loop.

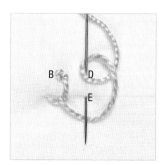

9 Slip the loop off your thumb and onto the fabric, keeping the needle within it. Take the needle from D–E.

10 Pull the thread through as before to complete the second stitch.

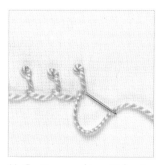

11 Continue working stitches in the same manner. After the last stitch, take the needle to the back just over the last loop.

12 Pull the thread through and secure on the back.

# BLANKET STITCH – LONG AND SHORT

1 Secure the thread on the back of the fabric and bring it to the front at A.

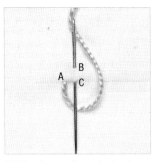

2 Take the needle to the back at B and emerge at C. Ensure the thread is under the tip of the needle.

3 Pull the thread through until it lies snugly against the emerging thread but does not distort the fabric.

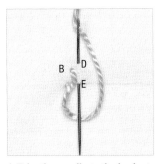

4 Take the needle to the back at D and emerge at E. This is parallel to the previous stitch but longer. Ensure the thread lies under the tip of the needle.

5 Pull the thread through as before.

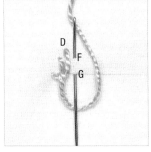

6 Take the needle to the back at F and emerge at G to make a stitch the same length as the first. Ensure the thread lies under the tip of the needle.

7 Pull the thread through as before.

8 Take the needle to the back at H and emerge at I to make a stitch the same length as the second. Ensure the thread lies under the tip of the needle.

9 Pull the thread through as before.

10 Continue working stitches in the same manner.

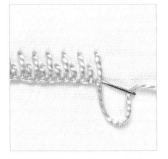

11 To finish, take the needle to the back of the fabric just over the last loop.

12 Pull the thread through and secure on the back.

# BLANKET STITCH – PINWHEEL

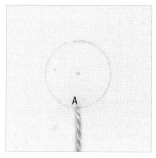

1 Draw a circle and mark the centre. Secure the thread on the back of the fabric and bring it to the front at A.

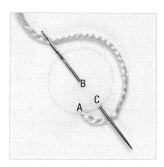

2 Take the needle to the back at B and emerge at C. Ensure the thread is under the tip of the needle.

3 Pull the thread through until it lies snugly against the emerging thread but does not distort the fabric.

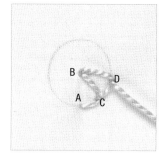

4 Take the needle to the back at B and emerge at D. Ensure the thread lies under the tip of the needle. Pull the thread through as before.

5 Continue working stitches around the circle in the same manner, turning the fabric as you go.

6 To finish, take the needle from B to A. Ensure the thread is under the tip of the needle.

7 Pull the thread through. Take the needle to the back just over the loop.

8 Pull the thread through and secure on the back.

# BLANKET STITCH – PARTIAL PINWHEEL

1 Secure the thread on the back of the fabric and bring it to the front at A.

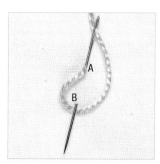

2 Take the needle to the back at A and emerge at B. Ensure the thread is under the tip of the needle.

3 Pull the thread through until it lies snugly against the emerging thread but does not distort the fabric.

4 Take the needle to the back at A and emerge at C. Ensure the thread lies under the tip of the needle.

## BLANKET STITCH – PARTIAL PINWHEEL *CONTINUED*

**5** Pull the thread through as before.

**6** Continue working the required number of stitches, beginning each one at A and fanning them at the outer edge.

**7** To finish, take the needle to the back just over the last loop.

**8** Pull the thread through and secure on the back.

# BLANKET STITCH – SAWTOOTH

**1** Secure the thread on the back of the fabric and bring it to the front at A.

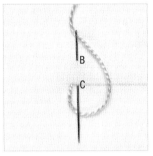

**2** Take the needle to the back at B and emerge at C. Ensure the thread is under the tip of the needle.

**3** Pull the thread through until it lies snugly against the emerging thread but does not distort the fabric.

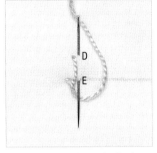

**4** Take the needle to the back at D and emerge at E. Ensure the thread is under the tip of the needle.

**5** Pull the thread through as before to work a second stitch exactly the same as the first.

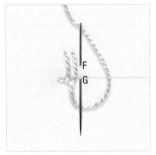

**6** Take the needle to the back at F and emerge at G to make a short stitch. Ensure the thread lies under the tip of the needle.

**7** Pull the thread through as before.

**8** Take the needle to the back at H and emerge at I to make a stitch the same length as the previous stitch. Ensure the thread lies under the tip of the needle.

**9** Pull the thread through as before.

**10** Continue working stitches in the same manner, always working two long and then two short stitches.

**11** To finish, take the needle to the back of the fabric just over the last loop.

**12** Pull the thread through and secure on the back.

## Norfolk Chronicle

**17 February 1780**

A.S. ALDERTON having opened a Boarding and Day School, at Beccles in Suffolk, presents her respectful Compliments to the Ladies and Gentlemen in Beccles and its Environs, and likewise to her Friends in Ipswich and Yarmouth, and begs Leave to acquaint them and the Public in general, that her House, (situated between the Church-Yard and the Market-Place) is now ready for the Reception of Boarders and Day-Scholars.

Her Terms are, Parlour Boarders, 21 Pounds per Ann. Entrance 2 Pound 2 Shillings. Boarders, fourteen Guineas and one Guinea Entrance, Tea, Sugar and Washing excepted: to bring with them a half Dozen breakfast Napkins.

The strictest Attention will be paid to the Morals of those Pupils committed to her Care, and to every Part of their Education. Tambour, Dresden, Dearning, Plain Work, etc at Eight Shillings per Quarter.

# BRAID STITCH

*For clarity, this stitch is shown worked wider than normal.*

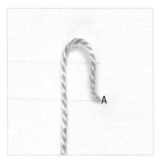

1 Bring the thread to the front at A on the lower line. Loop the thread to the left of A.

2 Fold the loop over so the working thread crosses behind the emerging thread.

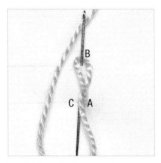

3 Holding the loop with your thumb, insert the needle through the loop at B on the upper line. Emerge at C, directly below on the lower line.

4 Loop the thread from right to left under the tip of the needle.

5 Pull the loop tightly around the needle.

6 Pull the thread through in a downward motion.

7 Make a second loop following steps 1 and 2.

8 Insert the needle through the loop and into the fabric on the upper line. Emerge on the lower line. Loop the thread to the left under the needle as before.

9 Pull the thread through to complete the second stitch.

10 Continue working stitches in the same manner.

11 To finish, take the needle to the back of the fabric just below the last loop of thread.

12 Pull the thread through and secure on the back.

# BRICK STITCH

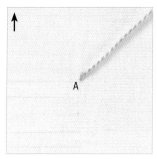

1 **Horizontal stitches** Secure the thread on the back of the fabric and bring it to the front at A, on the right hand side.

2 Work running stitch (see page 40) across the row, keeping the stitches the same length on the front as on the back.

3 After completing the row, turn the fabric upside down.

4 Work running stitch between the stitches of the previous row, using the same holes in the fabric.

5 Work all remaining rows in the same manner.

6 **Vertical stitches** Bring the thread to the front through the fabric hole shared by the first and second running stitches in the first row.

7 Take the needle to the back through the fabric hole shared by the first and second running stitches in the second row.

8 Emerge through the fabric hole shared by the first and second running stitches in the third row.

9 Pull the thread through.

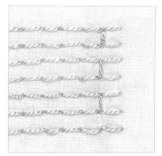

10 Continue working stitches to the last horizontal row in the same manner.

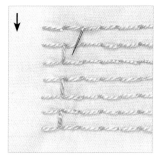

11 Turn the fabric upside down. Bring the needle to the front through the fabric hole shared by the second and third stitches in the first row.

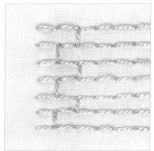

12 Work stitches in every alternate row in the same manner as before. These stitches are in the adjacent rows to the previous line of stitches.

## BRICK STITCH *CONTINUED*

13 Turn the fabric. Bring the needle to the front through the fabric hole shared by the third and fourth stitches in the first row.

14 Work a third row in the same manner as the first row.

15 Continue working lines of stitches in the same manner.

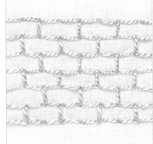

16 After the last stitch, secure on the back.

# BULLION KNOT

↑ indicates top of fabric

1 Secure the thread on the back of the fabric and bring it to the front at A.

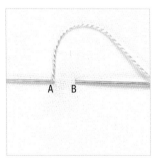

2 Take the needle to the back at B. Emerge at A, taking care not to split the thread.

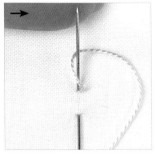

3 Rotate the fabric. Raise the tip of the needle away from the fabric. Wrap the thread clockwise around the needle.

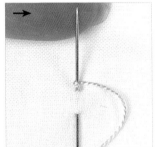

4 Keeping the tip of the needle raised, pull the wrap firmly down onto the fabric.

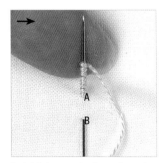

5 Add the required number of wraps. The number of wraps must cover the distance from A–B plus 1–2 wraps. Keep the wraps even.

6 Keeping tension on the wraps with your thumb, begin to ease the needle through the fabric and wraps.

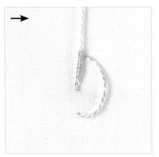

7 Continuing to keep tension on the wraps with your thumb, pull the thread through.

8 Pull the thread all the way through, tugging it away from you to form a small pleat in the fabric. This helps to ensure a tight even knot.

## BULLION KNOT *CONTINUED*

9 Release the thread. Smooth out the fabric and the knot will lie back towards B.

10 To ensure all the wraps are even, gently stroke and manipulate them with the needle while maintaining tension on the thread.

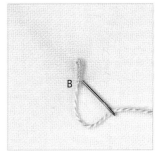

11 To finish, take the needle to the back at B.

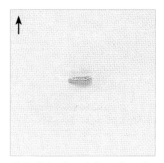

12 Pull the thread through and secure on the back.

# CABLE CHAIN STITCH

1 Secure the thread on the back of the fabric and bring it to the front at A, on the right hand side.

2 Take the thread over then under the needle in a clockwise direction.

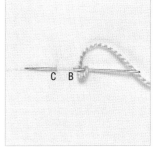

3 Take the needle through the fabric from B–C.

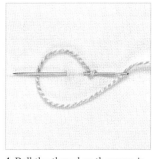

4 Pull the thread so the wrap is firm around the needle. Take the thread counterclockwise under the tip of the needle.

5 Pull the thread through.

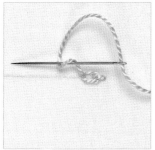

6 Take the thread over then under the needle in a clockwise direction.

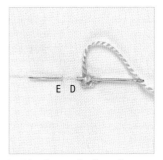

7 Take the needle through the fabric from D–E.

8 Pull the thread so it is firm around the needle. Take the thread counterclockwise under the tip of the needle.

9 Pull the thread through.

10 Continue working stitches in the same manner.

11 After the last stitch take the needle to the back over the loop.

12 Pull the thread through and secure on the back.

# CABLE PLAIT STITCH

*For clarity this stitch is shown worked wider than normal.*

1 Rule two parallel lines. Secure the thread on the back of the fabric and bring it to the front at A, at the top of the left hand line.

2 Hold the thread taut in your left hand and take the needle from right to left under the thread. Do not go through the fabric.

3 Twist the tip of the needle back over the thread in a counterclockwise direction.

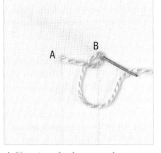

4 Keeping the loop on the needle, take the needle to the back at B, at the top of the right hand line.

5 Pull the thread through, leaving a loop on the front.

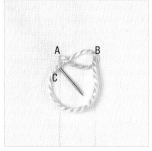

6 Bring the needle to the front at C, inside the new loop and just below A.

7 Pull the loop taut around the tip of the needle.

8 Pull the thread through.

# CABLE PLAIT STITCH CONTINUED

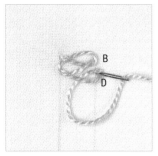

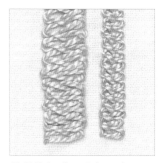

**9** Hold the thread to the left. Twist the tip of the needle around the thread in the same manner as before. Take the needle to the back at D just below B.

**10** Complete the stitch in the same manner as before.

**11** Continue working stitches in the same manner. To finish, take the needle to the back just to the left of the last loop.

**12** Pull the thread through and secure on the back.

*Mountmellick doiley*

# CHAIN STITCH - ROSETTE

*For clarity this stitch is shown worked wider than normal.*

1 Secure the thread on the back of the fabric and bring it to the front at A, on the right hand end.

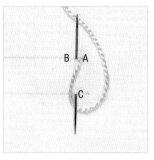

2 Take the needle through the fabric from B–C. Wrap the thread, from left to right, under the tip of the needle.

3 Pull the loop taut and hold in place with your left thumb.

4 Keeping your thumb over the loop, pull the needle and thread through.

5 Slide the needle from right to left under the right hand section of thread. Do not go through the fabric.

6 Begin to pull the thread through.

7 Pull until the loop rests alongside the previous loop.

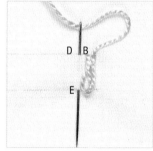

8 To begin the second stitch, insert the needle at D and emerge at E.

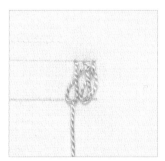

9 Loop the thread counter-clockwise around the tip of the needle and pull through as before.

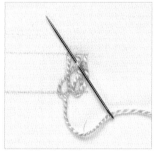

10 Slide the needle from right to left under the section of thread between the stitches.

11 Pull the thread through to complete the stitch. Continue working stitches in the same manner.

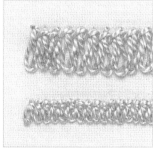

12 To finish, take the thread to the back just to the left of the top of the last stitch. Secure on the back.

# CHAIN STITCH – TWISTED

1 Secure the thread on the back of the fabric and bring it to the front at A.

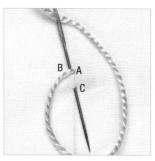

2 Take the needle to the back at B, just to the left of A. Emerge at C, directly below A.

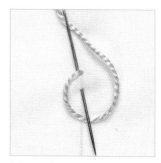

3 Loop the thread from left to right under the tip of the needle.

4 Pull the thread through until the loop lies snugly against the emerging thread.

5 Take the needle to the back at D, just to the left of the previous loop. Emerge at E. Loop the thread as before.

6 Pull the thread through. Continue working stitches in the same manner.

7 To finish, take the needle to the back just under the last loop.

8 Pull the thread through and secure on the back of the fabric.

# CHAIN STITCH – WHIPPED

1 Work a line of chain stitch following the instructions on page 9.

2 Secure a new thread on the back and bring it to the front halfway along the left hand side of the first chain stitch.

3 Slide the needle from right to left behind the second chain stitch. Do not go through the fabric.

4 Pull the thread through until it lies gently against the chain stitch.

## CHAIN STITCH – WHIPPED *CONTINUED*

5 Slide the needle from right to left behind the third chain stitch. Again, do not go through the fabric.

6 Pull the thread through. Continue whipping stitches in the same manner to the end of the chain stitches.

7 To finish, take the needle to the back of the fabric behind the last stitch.

8 Pull the thread through and secure on the back.

# CORAL STITCH – ZIGZAG

1 Mark two lines on the fabric. Secure the thread on the back and bring it to the front at A, at the top of the left hand line.

2 Lay the thread diagonally towards the right and hold in place. Loop the thread to the left.

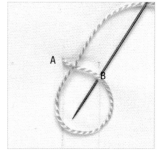

3 Take the needle to the back at B, on the right hand line. Emerge within the loop of thread.

4 Begin to pull the thread through ensuring the loop is under the tip of the needle.

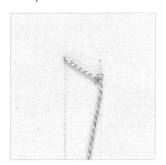

5 Pull until a knot forms.

6 Lay the thread diagonally towards the left and hold in place. Loop the thread to the right.

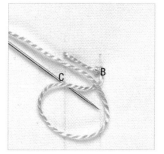

7 Take the needle to the back at C, on the left hand line. Emerge within the loop of thread.

8 Begin to pull the thread through ensuring the loop of thread is under the tip of the needle.

## CORAL STITCH – ZIGZAG *CONTINUED*

9 Pull until a second knot forms.

10 Alternating from side to side, continue working stitches to the end of the line in the same manner.

11 To finish, take the needle to the back, just after the last knot.

12 Pull the thread through and secure on the back.

# CORDING STITCH

*For clarity this stitch is shown worked wider than normal.*

1 Secure the thread on the back of the fabric and bring it to the front at A on the left hand side.

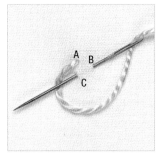

2 Take the needle through the fabric diagonally from B to C. Ensure the thread is under the tip of the needle.

3 Pull the thread through until it lies snugly against the emerging thread but does not distort the fabric.

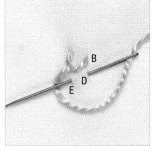

4 Take the needle from D to E. Ensure the thread lies under the tip of the needle.

5 Pull the thread through as before.

6 Continue working stitches in the same manner.

7 To finish, take the needle to the back of the fabric just over the last loop.

8 Pull the thread through and secure on the back.

# COUCHING – BOKHARA

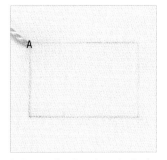

1 Secure the thread on the back of the fabric and bring it to the front at A on the left hand side of the shape.

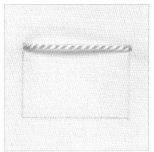

2 Take the thread to the back on the right hand side. Pull the thread through to form a long straight stitch.

3 Bring the needle to the front just under the straight stitch a short distance from the right hand end.

4 Pull the thread through. Take the needle to the back just above the straight stitch and a little to the left of where it emerged.

5 Pull the thread through. Bring the needle to the front just under the straight stitch a little further towards the left.

6 Pull the thread through. Take it to the back in the same manner as before to form a second short diagonal stitch.

7 Continue working little diagonal stitches in the same manner to the end of the long straight stitch.

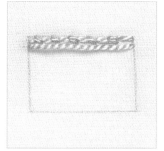

8 Bring the needle to the front just below the end of the first laid thread. Work a long straight stitch directly below the first.

9 Emerge below this second straight stitch approx-imately the same distance from the edge as before.

10 Take the needle to the back between the two straight stitches and just to the left of where it emerged.

11 Continue working couching and foundation stitches in the same manner.

12 After working the last couching stitch, take the thread to the back and secure.

# COUCHING – ROUMANIAN

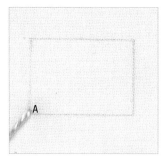

1 Secure the thread on the back of the fabric and bring it to the front at A on the left hand side of the shape.

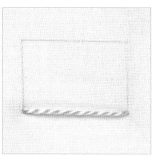

2 Take the thread to the back on the right hand side. Pull the thread through to form a long straight stitch.

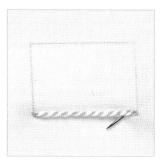

3 Bring the needle to the front just under the straight stitch.

4 Pull the thread through. Take the needle to the back just above the straight stitch and to the left of where it emerged.

5 Pull the thread through until this stitch lies on the horizontal stitch. Bring the needle to the front just under the straight stitch a little further to the left.

6 Pull the thread through. Take the needle to the back in the same manner as before to form a second diagonal stitch.

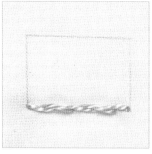

7 Complete the couching stitch as before.

8 Bring the needle to the front just above the end of the first laid thread. Work a long straight stitch directly above the first.

9 Emerge between the two long straight stitches.

10 Take the needle to the back just above the straight stitch and to the left of where it emerged. Pull the thread through.

11 Continue working couching and foundation stitches in the same manner.

12 After working the last couching stitch, take the thread to the back and secure.

# CRETAN STITCH

1  Rule four lines on the fabric to help with stitch placement. Secure the thread on the back of the fabric and bring it to the front at A, at the top of the first line.

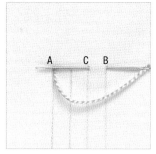

2  Take the needle from B to C. Ensure the thread is below the needle.

3  Pull the thread through.

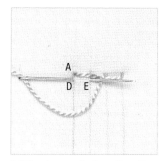

4  Take the needle from D to E. Ensure the thread is under the tip of the needle.

5  Pull the thread through until it lies snugly against the emerging thread.

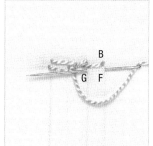

6  Take the needle from F to G. Ensure the thread is under the tip of the needle.

7  Pull the thread through until it lies snugly against the emerging thread.

8  Continue working stitches in the same manner, alter-nating from right to left.

9  To finish, take the needle to the back of the fabric just below the last stitch very close to where it emerged.

10  Pull the thread through and secure on the back.

11  Cretan stitch with the stitches spaced apart.

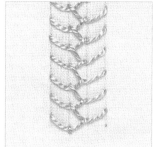

12  Cretan stitch worked with the needle angled.

# FEATHER STITCH – CLOSED

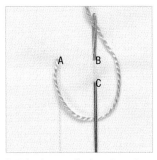

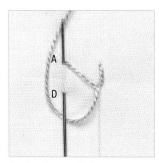

**1** Rule two parallel lines. Secure the thread on the back and bring it to the front at A, on the left hand line.

**2** Take the needle from B to C, on the right hand line. Loop the thread under the tip of the needle.

**3** Pull the thread through, in a downward motion, until the loop rests against the emerging thread.

**4** Take the needle from A to D, using the same hole in the fabric at A. Loop the thread under the tip of the needle.

**5** Pull the thread through as before.

**6** Continue working stitches in the same manner, alter-nating from side to side.

**7** After the last stitch, take the needle to the back of the fabric just below the loop.

**8** Pull the thread through and secure on the back.

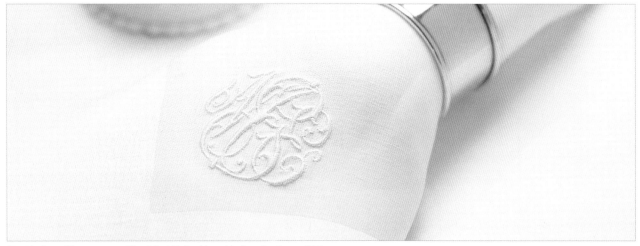

*Napkin from Monograms – The Art of Embroidered Letters by Susan O'Connor*

# FEATHER STITCH – SPANISH KNOTTED

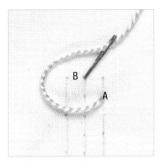

1 Rule three parallel lines. Secure the thread on the back and bring it to the front at A. Loop the thread to the left and take the needle to the back at B.

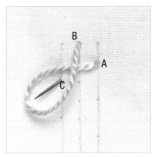

2 Twist the thread to form a loop. Gently pull the thread through to form a smaller loop. Bring the needle to the front at C, inside the circle.

3 Keeping your left thumb on the loop, pull the thread through until the looped thread rests against the emerging thread.

4 Take the needle to the back at D, level with A and on the middle line. Loop the thread in a clockwise direction.

5 Begin to pull the thread through leaving a loop on the front. Bring the needle to the front at E inside the loop of thread.

6 Pull the thread through until the looped thread rests against the emerging thread.

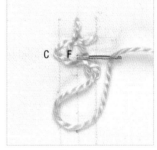

7 Loop the thread to the left. Take the needle to the back at F, level with C and on the middle line.

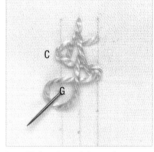

8 Pull the thread through leaving a small loop on the front. Emerge at G, inside the loop of thread.

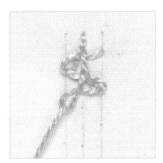

9 Pull the thread through until the looped thread rests against the emerging thread.

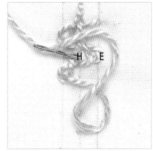

10 Loop the thread below the last stitch. Take the needle to the back at H, level with E and on the middle line.

11 Begin to pull the thread through leaving a loop on the front. Emerge inside the loop at I, on the right hand line.

12 Pull the thread through until the looped thread rests against the emerging thread.

## FEATHER STITCH – SPANISH KNOTTED *CONTINUED*

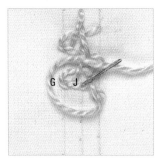

**13** Loop the thread to the left. Take the needle to the back at J, level with G, and on the middle line.

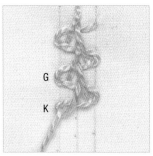

**14** Emerge inside the loop at K, on the left hand line. Pull the thread through until the looped thread rests against the emerging thread.

**15** Continue working stitches in the same manner. After working the last stitch, take the needle to the back just over the last loop.

**16** Pull the thread through and secure on the back.

# FERN STITCH

**1** Draw a line on the fabric. Bring the thread to the front at A, a short distance from the end of the line.

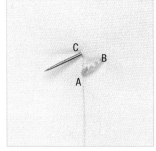

**2** Take the thread to the back at B, on the right hand side, and emerge at C, at the end of the line.

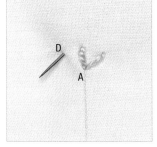

**3** Pull the thread through. Take the thread to the back at A and emerge at D, on the left hand side.

**4** Pull the thread through. Take the needle to the back at A.

**5** Pull the thread through to complete the first stitch.

**6** Bring the thread to the front at E, on the marked line.

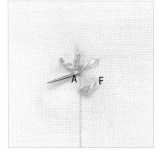

**7** Take the thread to the back at F, on the right hand side, and emerge at A, through the same hole in the fabric.

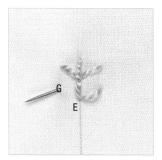

**8** Pull the thread through. Take the needle to the back at E and emerge at G, on the left hand side.

9 Pull the thread through. Take the needle to the back at E.

10 Pull the thread through to complete the second stitch.

11 Continue working in the same manner.

12 Secure on the back.

# FLAKE STITCH

*Flake stitch is worked in a similar manner to the soft shading used in crewel embroidery, but of course, the thread colour does not change.*

1 Mark the shape to be filled on the fabric. Secure the thread on the back and bring it to the front at A, on the outline.

2 Work a series of straight stitches around the outer edge working one long and then one short stitch.

3 To begin the second row, bring the needle to the front, splitting a stitch of the previous row.

4 Pull the thread through and make a stitch that extends beyond the first row of stitches.

5 Continue working stitches in the same manner, varying the length of the stitches and keeping them close together so no fabric shows through.

6 Work all subsequent rows in the same manner as the second row.

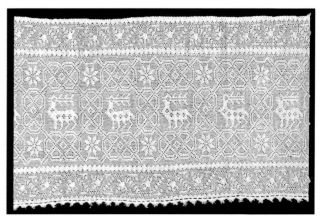

*Punto Tirato – Sicilian cut and drawn thread work, 17th century*

# GORDIAN KNOT STITCH

1 Secure the thread on the back of the fabric and bring it to the front at A, on the right hand side.

2 Hold the thread along the line. Slide the needle from top to bottom under the thread. Do not go through the fabric.

3 Lift the thread with your needle.

4 Take the needle into the fabric at the position for the knot, picking up 1 to 2 threads of the fabric. Pull the thread so the wrap is firm around the needle.

5 Take the thread from right to left under the needle and hold in place.

6 Begin to pull the thread through, pulling in a down-ward direction.

7 When the circle of thread is small, pull the thread to the left.

8 Hold the thread to the left and loop it clockwise.

9 Slide the needle under the thread as before.

10 Complete the stitch following steps 3–8.

11 Continue working stitches in the same manner. To finish, take the needle to the back just to the left of the last knot.

12 Pull the thread through and secure on the back.

# HONEYCOMB STITCH

1 Secure the thread on the back of the fabric and bring it to the front at A.

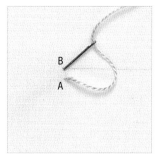

2 Take the needle to the back at B, approximately 3mm (⅛") above A.

3 Pull the thread through to form a vertical straight stitch. Bring the needle to the front at A.

4 Pull the thread through. Work blanket stitch across the row, spacing the stitches approx 3mm (⅛") apart (see page 32) and keeping the loops slightly loose.

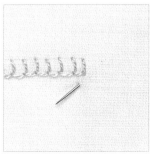

5 Take the thread just over the last loop to anchor it. Bring the needle to the front approx 3mm (⅛") below the centre of the last loop.

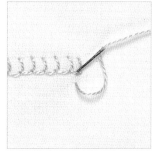

6 Pull the thread through. Take the needle to the back over the last loop.

7 Pull the thread through to form a straight stitch. Emerge at the base of the straight stitch.

8 Loop the thread to the left. Take the needle to the back over the centre of the next loop to the left and emerge 3mm (⅛") below.

9 Ensure the thread is under the tip of the needle.

10 Pull the thread through to form a blanket stitch.

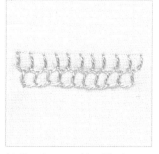

11 Continue working blanket stitches from right to left across the row in the same manner.

12 To begin the third row, work a vertical straight stitch.

## HONEYCOMB STITCH *CONTINUED*

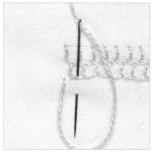 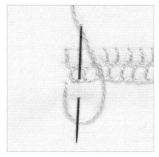  

13 Take the needle to the back over the centre of the last loop in the previous row. Emerge 3mm (⅛") below.

14 Ensure the thread is under the tip of the needle.

15 Work blanket stitches, from left to right, across the row. Ensure the vertical section of each stitch lies over the centre of a loop in the previous row.

16 Continue working back and forth for the desired number of rows. Secure the thread on the back.

# KNITTED FRINGE – MAKING A SLIP KNOT

*We have used two strands of cotton pearl for photographic purposes.*

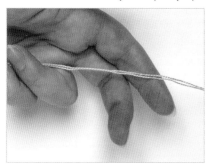 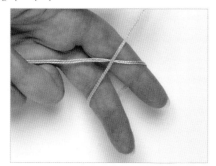 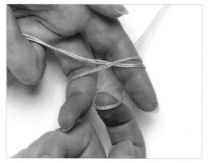

1 Place the ends of 3 to 4 strands of cotton together. Hold the ends of the thread across the palm of your hand with your third and fourth fingers.

2 Wrap the threads around your first and second fingers, as shown.

3 Spread your first and second fingers and take the threads between your fingers and through the loop. A new loop will form.

 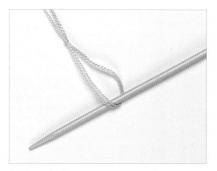 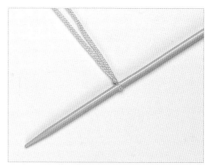

4 Pull the loop of threads through to tighten the knot.

5 Place this loop onto your needle.

6 Tighten the loop on your needle by pulling on the threads.

# KNITTED FRINGE – CASTING ON

1 With the slip knot on your left needle, insert the tip of your right needle through the loop, taking it behind the left needle.

2 Take the thread from the back to the front, around the tip of the right needle.

3 Pull the thread down between your two needles until it rests on the loop.

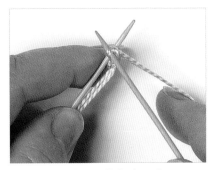

4 Draw the right needle back so the slip knot glides to the tip. As you reach the tip, angle the needle to pick up the thread between.

5 Pull the thread through, forming a loop on the right needle.

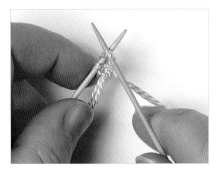

6 Hook the new loop over the left needle.

## Pina cloth embroidery

Filipino girls were introduced to European embroidery during the time that the Philippines were a Spanish colony. Embroidery was taught in the convents and schools, and this still continues today.

Traditionally this floral embroidery was worked on pina cloth – a fine translucent fabric that was made from pineapple fibres. Today cotton fabric is more commonly used.

*Pina cloth, circa 1890*

## KNITTED FRINGE – CASTING ON *CONTINUED*

**7** Remove the right needle from the loop. There are now two loops (or stitches) on the left needle.

**8** Take the right needle from front to back between the two stitches. Pull the thread to tighten.

The length of the fringe is determined by the number of stitches left on the needle. Increase or decrease as required but ensure that there is an odd number.

**9** Repeat steps 2 to 8 to complete the third stitch.

**10** Continue working the required number of stitches, ensuring it is a multiple of three, in the same manner. We used twelve stitches.

### Whitework for the White House

President Kennedy was presented with a Mountmellick 'white quilt for the White House' during his visit to Ireland in 1963.

# KNITTED FRINGE – KNITTING

**1** After casting on the stitches, hold the needle with the stitches in the left hand. Hold the empty needle with the right hand.

**2** Insert the tip of the needle through the front of the first stitch.

**3** Wrap the thread from back to front between the tips of the needles.

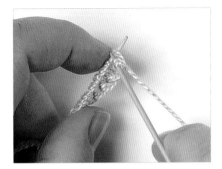

4 Draw the tip of the needle back through the stitch on the left needle. Keep the wrapped thread on the right needle.

5 The wrapped thread will form a new stitch on the right needle.

6 Slide the needle to the right, slipping the used loop on the tip of the left needle off the needle.

7 Bring the thread to the front between the tips of the needles.

8 Take the right needle through the front of the next two stitches.

9 Wrap the thread around the tip of the right needle.

10 Draw the tip back through the stitches, keeping the new stitch on the right needle as before.

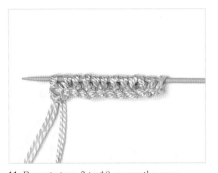

11 Repeat steps 2 to 10 across the row.

12 Continue working rows in the same manner until the knitting is long enough to go around your embroidery without stretching.

# KNITTED FRINGE – CASTING OFF

1 Hold the needle with the stitches in the left hand. Knit the first two stitches.

2 Take the tip of the left needle from left to right behind the front of the first stitch on the right needle.

3 Take the stitch over the second stitch and off the right needle.

4 Slip the tip of the left needle out of the stitch so it drops below the one stitch remaining on the right needle.

5 Knit the next stitch.

6 Repeat steps 2 to 4 to cast off the next stitch.

7 Continue in this manner until there are five stitches on the left needle and one stitch on the right.

8 Cut the thread, leaving a 10cm (4") tail. Loosen the stitch on the right needle and remove the needle. Thread the tail through the loop.

9 Pull the tail firmly to tighten the loop.

# KNITTED FRINGE – UNRAVELLING

1 Hold the cast off end in your left hand and remove the remaining needle.

2 Place the knitting needle in the first stitch of the uncast off section and pull it out.

3 Repeat for all remaining stitches along the entire length of the knitting.

# KNITTED FRINGE – ATTACHING THE FRINGE

*Attach the fringe using a strand of the same thread that was used for knitting.*

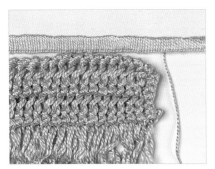

1 Secure the thread on the back of the fabric and bring it to the front near the edge. With right sides facing, butt the blanket stitch edge and fringe together.

2 Take the needle behind one blanket stitch loop and then from back to front through the first knot on the edge of the knitting.

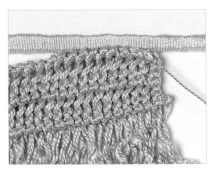

3 Pull the thread through.

4 Take the needle behind the blanket stitch loop in line with the next knot on the edge of the knitting and through that knot in the same manner as before.

5 Pull the thread through. Continue in the same manner until the entire fringe is attached to the edging.

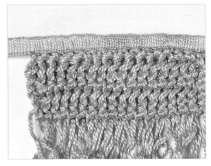

6 End off the thread on the back of the fabric.

# LOOP STITCH

1 Draw two lines on the fabric. Secure the thread on the back and bring it to the front at A, halfway between the lines on the right hand end.

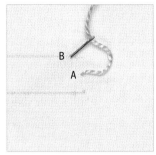

2 Take the needle to the back at B, slightly to the left of A and on the upper line.

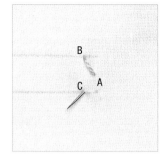

3 Pull the thread through. Bring the needle to the front at C, directly below B on the lower line.

4 Pull the thread through. Loop the thread to the left.

5 Slide the needle from right to left under the diagonal stitch. Ensure the tip is over the looped thread.

6 Pull the thread through. Ensure the wrap is halfway between the marked lines. Take the needle to the back at D to begin the second stitch.

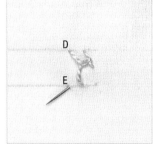

7 Pull the thread through. Bring the needle to the front at E, directly below D on the lower line.

8 Pull the thread through. Loop the thread and slide the needle in the same manner as before.

9 Pull the thread through ensuring the wrap lies halfway between the marked lines.

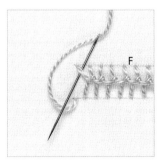

10 Continue working stitches from right to left in the same manner.

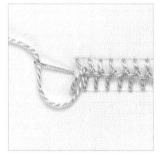

11 After working the last stitch, take the needle to the back halfway between the two lines and to the left of the stitch.

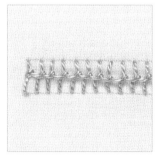

12 Pull the thread through and secure on the back.

# MOUNTMELLICK STITCH

1  Draw a line on the fabric. Secure the thread on the back and bring it to the front at A, at the top of the line.

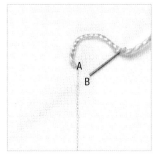

2  Take the needle to the back at B.

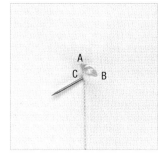

3  Pull the thread through and emerge at C.

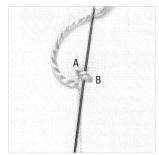

4  Pull the thread through. Take the needle through the stitch. Do not go through the fabric.

5  Pull the thread through. Loop the thread to the left, and take the needle to the back at A.

6  Pull the thread through, leaving a loop on the front.

7  Bring the needle to the front at C. Ensure it is inside the loop.

8  Pull the thread through until the loop lies snugly against the emerging thread.

9  Take the needle to the back at D.

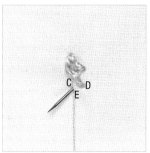

10  Pull the thread through and emerge at E.

11  Pull the thread through. Take the needle through the stitch in the same manner as before.

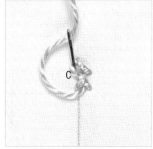

12  Pull the thread through. Loop the thread to the left  and take the needle to the back at C.

## MOUNTMELLICK STITCH *CONTINUED*

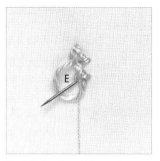

13 Pull the thread through, leaving a loop on the front. Bring the needle to the front at E inside the loop.

14 Pull the thread through until the loop lies snugly against the emerging thread.

15 Continue in the same manner to the end. After the last stitch, take the needle to the back just over the last loop.

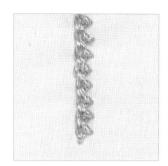

16 Pull the thread through and secure on the back.

# OVERCAST STITCH – INDENTED

1 Work a line of back stitch (see page 43) or close running stitch (see page 40) for padding.

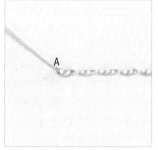

2 Secure a new thread on the back and bring it to the front at A, near one end of the padding.

3 Take the needle to the back directly opposite on the other side of the padding.

4 Pull the thread through to form a stitch that is at a right angle to the padding.

5 Emerge next to A.

6 Take the needle to the back directly opposite, but further away than the first stitch.

7 Pull the thread through.

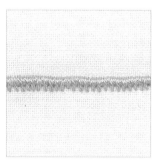

8 Continue, working one short stitch followed by one long stitch for the required length.

# PALESTRINA STITCH

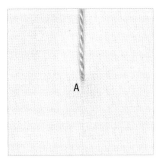

1 Draw a line on the fabric. Secure the thread on the back and bring it to the front at A.

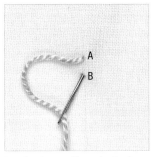

2 Take the needle to the back at B.

3 Pull the thread through.

4 Bring the needle to the front at C.

5 Pull the thread through. Slide the needle from right to left under the first stitch without going through the fabric.

6 Begin to pull the thread through.

7 Pull until the loop lies snugly around the first stitch.

8 Loop the thread and slide the needle from right to left under the first stitch, ensuring the loop is under the tip of the needle. Do not go through the fabric.

9 Gently pull the thread through to form a soft knot.

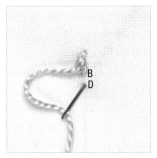

10 Take the needle to the back at D.

11 Pull the thread through. Bring the needle to the front at E.

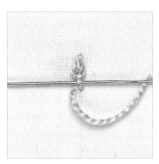

12 Pull the thread through. Slide the needle from right to left behind the second stitch. Do not go through the fabric.

# PALESTRINA STITCH *CONTINUED*

**13** Pull the thread through. Loop the thread and slide the needle under the second stitch as before. Ensure the loop is under the tip of the needle.

**14** Pull the thread through. Continue working stitches in the same manner.

**15** To finish, take the needle to the back of the fabric just below the last knot.

**16** Pull the thread through and secure on the back.

*Bed linen from Monograms – The Art of Embroidered Letters by Susan O'Connor*

# POINT DE REPRISE STITCH

1 Secure the thread on the back of the fabric and bring it to the front at A.

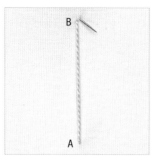

2 Take the needle to the back at B. Pull the thread through and emerge just next to B.

3 Pull the thread through and take it to the back just next to A.

4 Work two more straight stitches.

5 Bring the needle to the front alongside the end of the first straight stitch.

6 Pull the thread through. Take the needle from left to right over the first two threads and under the second two. Do not go through the fabric.

7 Pull the thread through. Push the thread close to the ends of the straight stitches.

8 Take the needle from right to left over the first two threads and under the next two. Do not go through the fabric.

9 Pull the thread through. Push the thread close against the previous one.

10 Continue working back and forth across the straight stitches in the same manner, pushing the wraps close together.

11 When the straight stitches are covered, take the needle to the back of the fabric behind the stitches.

12 Pull the thread through and secure on the back.

# PORTUGUESE KNOTTED STEM STITCH

1 Secure the thread on the back of the fabric and bring it to the front at A.

2 Take the needle to the back at B and pull through to form a straight stitch.

3 Bring the needle to the front at C on the left side of the straight stitch.

4 Pull the thread through. With the thread above the needle, slide it from right to left under the straight stitch, emerging below C.

5 Begin to gently pull the thread through.

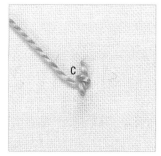

6 Pull the thread all the way through and up towards C. A wrap is formed around the straight stitch.

7 Keeping the thread above the needle, again slide the it from right to left under the straight stitch. Keep the needle below the first wrap.

8 Pull the thread through as before so a second wrap is formed below the first wrap.

9 To begin the second stitch, take the needle to the back at D.

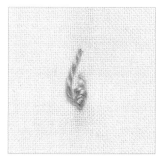

10 Pull the thread through.

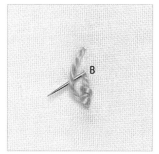

11 Bring the needle to the front at B.

12 Pull the thread through. Keeping the thread above the needle, slide it from right to left under both the first and second stitches.

## PORTUGUESE KNOTTED STEM STITCH *CONTINUED*

**13** Pull the thread through. Keeping the thread above the needle, slide it from right to left below the wrap just formed.

**14** Pull the thread through so a second wrap is formed.

**15** Continue in the same manner. After working the last stitch, take the needle to the back under the last wrap.

**16** Pull the thread through and secure on the back.

# SCROLL STITCH

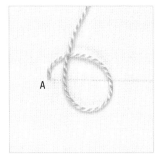

**1** Draw a line on the fabric. Secure the thread on the back and bring it to the front at A, on the left hand end.

**2** Make a loop to the right of A.

**3** Take the needle from B to C. Ensure the loop of thread lies under both ends of the needle.

**4** Pull the thread firmly so the loop tightens around the needle.

**5** Pull the needle and thread through to complete the first stitch.

**6** Loop the thread to the right and take a small stitch in exactly the same manner as before.

**7** Tighten the loop and pull the thread through. Continue in the same manner. After the last stitch, take the needle to the back of the fabric just below the loop.

**8** Pull the thread through and secure on the back.

# SEED STITCH

*It is important to maintain the correct pull on the thread. Work the stitches from right to left across the shape with the needle always pointing to the left.*

1 Secure the thread on the back of the fabric and bring it to the front at A.

2 Take the needle to the back at B.

3 Pull the thread through to form a tiny straight stitch.

4 Emerge next to A.

5 Pull the thread through. Take the needle to the back of the fabric next to B.

6 Pull the thread through to complete the first seed stitch.

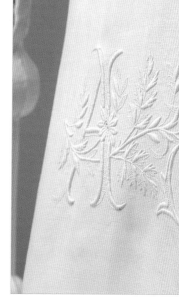

The Sheet from Monograms – The Art of Embroidered Letters by Susan O'Connor

7 Continue working stitches in the same manner until the required area is filled.

8 After completing the last stitch, secure the thread on the back.

135

# SPIDER WEB

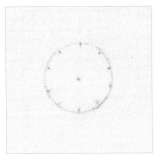

1 Draw a circle on the fabric and mark the centre with a dot. Mark the edge of the circle with evenly spaced dots.

2 **Framework** Secure the thread on the back of the fabric and bring it to the front at one dot on the edge.

3 Take the needle to the back at the centre.

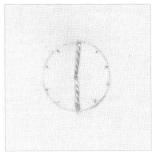

4 Pull the thread through. From the other side of the circle, work a second stitch to the centre.

5 Continue in the same manner until there is a straight stitch from each dot on the edge to the centre.

6 **Whipping** Bring the thread to the front between two spokes as close as possible to the centre.

7 Working in a clockwise direction, slide the needle under spokes 1 and 2. Do not go through the fabric.

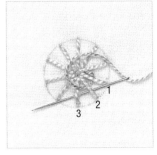

8 Firmly pull the thread through. Slide the needle under spokes 2 and 3. Do not go through the fabric.

9 Firmly pull the thread through. Continue (back one and under two) until one round is complete.

10 Continue in the same manner, gradually easing the tension as you spiral away from the centre.

11 Continue until the spokes are covered. Take the needle to the back of the fabric under the last spoke used.

12 Pull the thread through and secure on the back.

# STEM STITCH - WHIPPED

**1 Foundation** Work a line of stem stitch following the instructions on page 28.

**2 Whipping** Secure the thread on the back and bring it to the front at A, just above the first stem stitch.

**3** Slide the needle under the space shared by the first and second stem stitches. Do not go through the fabric.

**4** Pull the thread through.

**5** Slide the needle under the space shared by the second and third stitches. Do not go through the fabric.

**6** Pull the thread through. Continue to the end in the same manner.

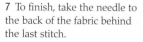

**7** To finish, take the needle to the back of the fabric behind the last stitch.

**8** Pull the thread through and secure on the back.

*Handkerchief with trailing from Monograms – The Art of Embroidered Letters by Susan O'Connor*

# THORN STITCH

1 Draw two parallel lines on the fabric. Secure the thread on the back and bring it to the front at A, at the top halfway between the lines.

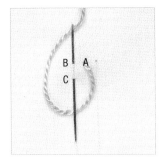

2 Take the needle to the back at B, on the left hand line, and emerge at C, a short distance below. Loop the thread under the needle tip.

3 Pull the thread through in a downward movement.

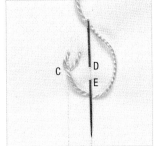

4 Take the needle from D to E on the right hand line. Loop the thread under the tip of the needle.

5 Pull the thread through in a downward movement.

6 Hold the thread down with your left thumb. Make three wraps on the needle as shown.

7 Turn the tip of the needle towards the fabric.

8 Take the needle to the back just above the loop of thread and emerge just below it.

9 Pull the wraps down to the fabric and take the thread from left to right under the tip of the needle.

10 Pull the thread through. A knot will form halfway between the two lines.

11 Continue working stitches in the same manner. After working the last knot, take the needle to the back of the fabric just below the knot.

12 Pull the thread through and secure on the back.

# VAN DYKE STITCH

1 Secure the thread on the back and bring it to the front at A, on the left hand side.

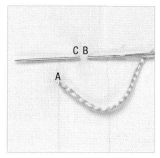

2 Take a small stitch from B to C, above and to the right of A.

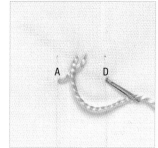

3 Pull the thread through. Take the needle to the back at D, directly opposite A.

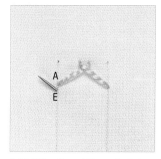

4 Pull the thread through. Bring the needle to the front at E, just below A.

5 Pull the thread through. Slide the needle from right to left behind the crossover point of the previous two stitches. Do not go through the fabric.

6 Pull the thread through. Take the needle to the back directly opposite E.

7 Pull the thread through. Continue working stitches in the same manner for the required distance.

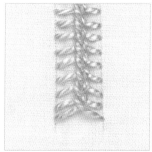

8 After working the last stitch, secure the thread on the back.

## Pattern books

Embroiderers did not create their own designs but relied heavily on the work of professional designers. These were either stamped onto the fabric or appeared in pattern books, which were being produced as early as the 16th century. An Italian book, *Giardineto novo di Punto* was published in 1566. It depicted geometric and floral motifs as well as two alphabets.

And how is this for a title – *New and Singular Patternes and workes of Linnen Serving for Patternes* to make all sorts of Lace Edgings and Cutworkes by Federico Vinciola, was printed in England in 1591.

# WAVE STITCH

1 Secure the thread on the back and bring it to the front at A on the left hand side.

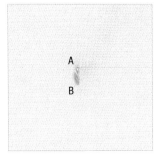

2 Take the thread to the back at B to form a small straight stitch.

3 Work parallel straight stitches across the top of the shape in the same manner, keeping them close together.

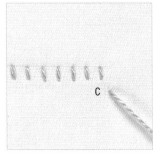

4 Bring the thread to the front at C, below the last straight stitch.

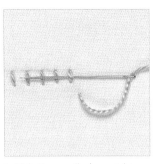

5 Slide the needle from right to left behind the last straight stitch. Do not go through the fabric.

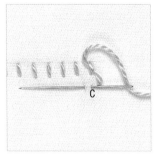

6 Pull the thread through. Pick up a tiny portion of fabric just to the left of C.

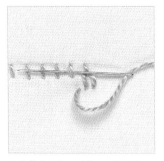

7 Pull the thread through. Take the needle through the next straight stitch in the same manner as before.

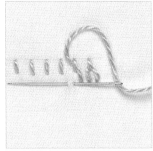

8 Pull the thread through and again, pick up a small portion of fabric just to the left of the previous stitch.

9 Pull the thread through. Continue in the same manner until the thread is looped through all the straight stitches.

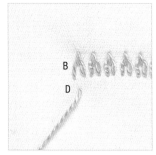

10 Take the thread to the back and emerge at D, directly below B.

11 Take the needle from left to right behind one half of each of the first two loops as shown.

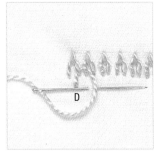

12 Pull the thread through. Pick up a tiny portion of fabric just to the right of D.

# WAVE STITCH CONTINUED

**13** Pull the thread through. Slide the needle from left to right behind one half of the second and third loops.

**14** Pull the thread through. Continue across the row in the same manner.

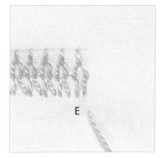

**15** Take the thread to the back and emerge directly below at E.

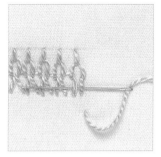

**16** Take the needle from right to left behind one half of each of the first two loops as shown.

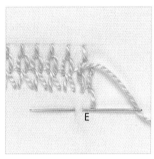

**17** Pull the thread through. Pick up a tiny portion of fabric just to the left of E.

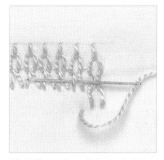

**18** Pull the thread through. Take the needle from right to left behind one half of the second and third loops.

**19** Pull the thread through. Continue across the row in the same manner.

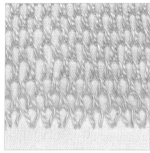

**20** Continue working rows back and forth across the shape until it is completely filled. Secure the thread on the back.

## Russian embroidery

The Archangel and Vologda districts of northern Russia are famous for their whitework, which is generally worked on white linen although occasionally square net is used.

Russian whitework is often used to decorate towels and sheets. The dense embroidery is worked in silk threads on a band of linen that is then attached to the towel or sheet with interlacing or hemstitch.

# WHEATEAR STITCH

1 Draw a line on the fabric. Secure the thread on the back and bring it to the front at A, to the left of the line.

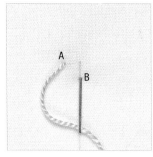

2 Take the needle to the back at B, on the line and diagonally below A.

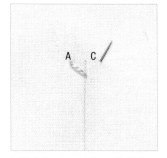

3 Pull the thread through. Bring the needle to the front at C, directly opposite A on the right hand side of the line.

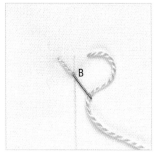

4 Pull the thread through. Take the needle to the back at B again.

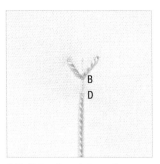

5 Pull the thread through. Emerge at D, directly below B on the marked line.

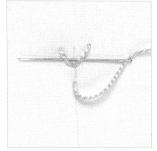

6 Slide the needle from right to left behind the previous two stitches. Do not go through the fabric.

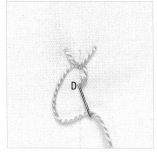

7 Pull the thread through and take the needle to the back at D.

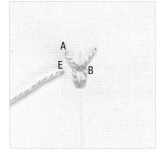

8 Pull the thread through. Emerge at E, directly below A and in line with B.

9 Work a straight stitch from E to D and then from F to D in the same manner as before.

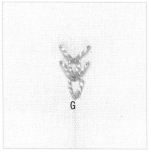

10 Bring the thread to the front at G and work a loop as before.

11 Continue working stitches down the line in the same manner.

12 Secure the thread on the back of the fabric after working the last straight stitch.

# Shadow work

## Also known as Etruscan work

Shadow work is delicate in appearance as it is worked on translucent fabrics that allow the thread at the back of the work to be visible. Stitch techniques are used that pass the thread from one side of the shape to the other, leaving a trail of thread between the surface stitches. The most common form of shadow work can be done in two ways – as double back stitch or as closed herringbone stitch. Both of these names belong to the same stitch; the difference being which side of the fabric they are worked from. Double back stitch is worked from the right side of the fabric and requires the design to be transferred to the front of the work. Closed herringbone is worked from the wrong side of the fabric and requires the reversed design to be transferred to the back of the work.

The length of the back stitches has a great impact on the appearance of the finished work – the shorter the stitches, the more solid the shadow will be. In Madeira embroidery, the stitching is done from the back and the stitches are so close that the thread on the back of the work forms a solid coverage giving the appearance of fabric from the front.

## HISTORY

References to shadow work appear in the folklore of both Persia (Iran) and India and as early as the 3rd century BC, Greek travellers wrote of such embroidery that they found in 'Indian' lands.

Chikankari or chikan embroidery is a form of delicate white work from Lucknow, Dacca and the Ganges plains of India that utilises shadow work in combination with pulled thread work and surface stitchery. In chikan work the shadow herringbone technique is known as 'Bakhia' or 'Bukhia' and is not always worked in exactly the same way as the western method. In some pieces it is worked as a simple zigzag stitch across the back of the motif and the thread does not cross over itself. European designs were worked in India to cater for the large British population and Indian whitework was often taken back to Europe where it was very highly prized.

The chikan work of Lucknow was considered the finest and indeed, won many prizes at international exhibitions in the 1880s. This tradition continues today with more than half a million inhabitants producing this work in Lucknow alone.

"In this embroidery, it is the effect of the threads showing through the ground fabric, rather than a particular stitch, that defines the work."

*Beth Gardner – The Sharp Needle*

Shadow work was also used extensively in Dresden embroidery, a beautiful form of whitework that reached its peak of popularity around 1750. Dresden work featured bold floral motives with pulled work fillings that were surrounded by shadow work borders. This precise and ornate form of embroidery was popular in Saxony in the mid 1700s with many of the designs being taken from brocaded silks that were woven in France.

Dresden work was designed to imitate lace and was also enormously popular in England and even found its way to America.

Contemporary shadow work is used extensively on babies' and children's clothing, the delicate appearance of the work being particularly suited to these garments. It is commonly used in conjunction with simple surface stitches – stem, outline, French knots and detached chain – to create pretty, dainty floral designs.

## MATERIALS

### Fabrics

This work requires a translucent fabric that allows the stitching on the back to shadow through. Fabrics such as handkerchief linen, organdie, voile, organza, batiste, chiffon and fine silk are the most suitable, but any fabric that has a translucent quality can be used. Wash and press the fabric before transferring the design.

### Threads

The most delicate finish will be achieved with a single strand of stranded cotton or silk. Fine pearl threads, broder spécial and floche are also suitable. Ensure that the thread is not too thick as this can result in the back of the fabric feeling bulky and lumpy.

### Needles

There are two distinct schools of thought on the correct needle for shadow embroidery: 1. a fine tapestry needle (no. 26–28), as the blunt tip prevents the splitting of the fabric threads. 2. a fine sharp or crewel needle (no. 10–12) allows the stitch to be positioned exactly where the embroiderer wants it. Try both and choose the one that you prefer. Change the needle size according to the thickness of the thread.

### Other

Mount the fabric in an embroidery hoop or frame to prevent it from puckering. Take extra care when beginning and ending a thread as the thread tails must be concealed beneath the surface stitches on the edge of the shape. Any threads that are run through the centre of the shape will be visible from the front.

*Italian shadow work doiley, circa 1900s*

## STITCHES FOR SHADOW WORK

Double back stitch
Closed herringbone stitch

144

# DOUBLE BACK STITCH

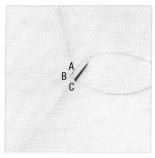

1  Begin with a waste knot. Work a stitch from A to B, on the upper line. Emerge at C on the lower side directly opposite A.

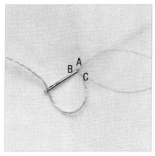

2  Pull the thread through. Take the needle to the back at B, using the same hole in the fabric as before.

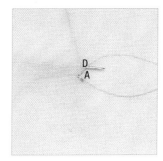

3  Pull the thread through. Emerge at D on the upper line and just beyond A.

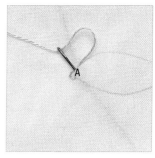

4  Pull the thread through. Take the needle to the back at A, using the same hole in the fabric as before.

5  Pull the thread through. Emerge at E on the lower line directly opposite D. Pull the thread through.

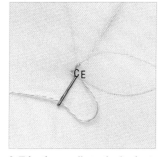

6  Take the needle to the back at C, using the same hole in the fabric as before.

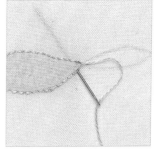

7  Pull the thread through. Continue in the same manner until reaching the crossover point. The last stitch on each line emerges at this point.

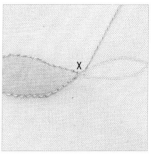

8  Pull the thread through. Bring the thread to the front on the opposite side just beyond the crossover point X.

9  Take the thread to the back at the crossover point using the same hole in the fabric as before. Emerge on the other line directly opposite X.

10  Pull the thread through. Take the needle to the back.

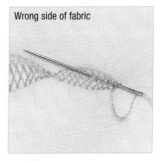

Wrong side of fabric

11  Pull the thread through and continue stitching in the same manner. Secure the thread on the back behind the back stitches.

12  Shadow work on the right side of the fabric.

# Tambour embroidery

## Also known as ari work

The title 'tambour embroidery' encompasses several styles of whitework that are all worked with a tambour hook or 'ari' that resembles a very fine crochet hook and is sometimes known as a crochet needle. Tambour embroidery takes its name from the frame on which it was worked and is French for 'drum'. This frame consists of two wooden hoops mounted on a curved wooden base that rests in the lap of the worker. The fabric is tightly stretched, like a drum, between the hoops, giving rise to the name.

In tambour embroidery the thread is held beneath the fabric with the left hand while the right hand holds the hook on the surface. The hook is used to pull the thread loops to the surface in a continuous line. The hook is inserted into the fabric then rotated 90 degrees to catch the thread. The hook is then pulled to the surface and the rotation is reversed to allow the new chain to be made.

The major attraction of this style of embroidery is the speed with which it is worked, enabling the embroiderer to produce large amounts of chain stitch in a relatively short time. It is also used to attach beads and sequins but has one major disadvantage in that it can be pulled out more quickly than it can be worked.

## HISTORY

This style of embroidery has been worked extensively in India and other parts of Asia for centuries and it is thought to have been brought to Europe from China around 1760.

Tambour embroidery enjoyed a long period of popularity between 1780 and 1850, a time in history known as the Romantic Era, and was primarily used to decorate fine, flowing white muslin gowns, net wedding veils and scarves. When fashionable taste turned towards more structured gowns in richly coloured silks, tamboured muslins and net were still used for veils, collars, fichus, cuffs and caps. After 1809, machine made net became widely available and there was a huge demand for tamboured and needlerun net laces.

Whilst it became exceedingly fashionable and was an easy and elegant accomplishment for stylish ladies, it was also a profitable commercial enterprise when worked on a large scale. Professional workshops were set up in Switzerland, Germany, Scotland, England and Ireland to produce endless lengths of embroidered fabric.

Rather than small areas being worked on a hoop, these workshops used large frames that could accommodate the entire width of the fabric and had several women working on them at once.

Madame de Pompadour had her portrait painted showing her working on a piece of tambour embroidery. In France, this style of work is known as Beauvais embroidery and is still widely used to produce commercial work.

## COGGESHALL EMBROIDERY

Coggeshall in Essex is the home of this form of white embroidery that was tamboured onto net and fine muslin. The development of this style of embroidery coincided with the opening of a silk mill in the town and the work was initially done onto silk net with silk thread. A French/Belgian immigrant Mr Drago, and his two daughters lived in the town and employed young embroiderers in a factory as well as older workers who completed the work in their homes.

This industry flourished in the first half of the 19th century and embroidery from this area is characterised by the use of wildflower motifs such as cow parsley, honeysuckle and other hedgerow flowers. Coggeshall embroidery was available for sale up until 1939.

"With a little practice, the stitches are made with marvellous rapidity."

*Ayrshire and Other Whitework, Margaret Swain*

## LIMERICK EMBROIDERY

Limerick embroidery, or lace as it is more commonly known, was established in 1829 by Charles Walker, an enterprising manufacturer who moved his business from England to Limerick in Ireland to take advantage of the cheap labour that was available. Lace work was best done by young females with nimble fingers who were easily controlled. Ireland offered a steady supply of such employees. Limerick embroidery was originally worked with a needle and used many of the same needlelace fillings as Carrickmacross work. The speedier tambour technique eventually took over and the fillings were no longer included. Designs consist mainly of trailing flower sprays with richly scalloped borders.

*Coggeshall lace flower and Limerick lace leaves, early 20th century*

## MATERIALS

### Fabrics

Tambour embroidery can be worked onto fine fabric or net but the fabric cannot be too finely woven or it will be difficult to pass the tambour hook back and forth through the surface. Cotton voile and batiste are suitable as are cotton and silk net. Tambour work can also be done on nylon net but the finish will be quite different to traditional work.

### Threads

High twist threads are preferable as they are less likely to untwist and be split by the hook. Size 30 or 50 cotton sewing thread is suitable for fine work. Linen lace thread is also suitable.

### Needles

A tambour hook is used and can be purchased with several hooks of varying sizes. The extra hooks are kept within the handle of the tool. Insert the desired hook into the holder aligning it with the screw so that you will always know which direction the hook is facing.

### Other

Tambour embroidery is worked in a hoop or frame. When working with net, take care not to stretch and distort the surface.

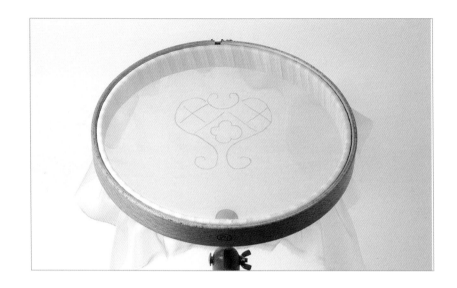

### STITCHES FOR TAMBOUR EMBROIDERY
Tambour chain stitch

# TAMBOUR CHAIN STITCH

*It is very important to secure the thread well at the beginning and end of the work. Keep the hook at a right angle to the fabric at all times.*

1 Holding the thread beneath the fabric, push the hook to the back.

2 Catch the thread onto the hook. Rotate the hook 90 degrees.

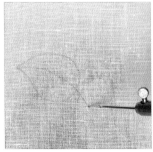

3 Pull the hook and the thread to the surface of the fabric.

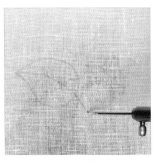

4 Rotate the hook 90 degrees in the opposite direction.

5 Adjust the thread from the back to control the loop size.

6 With the thread loop on the hook, push it to the back of the work.

7 Catch the thread, rotate the hook and return to the surface of the work.

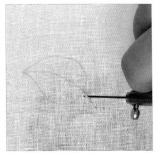

8 Rotate the hook in the opposite direction.

9 Continue working in this manner until the design is complete.

*Punto tirato – Sicilian cut and drawn thread work, 19th century*

# Index

# Acknowledgements

Special thanks to Christine P. Bishop for so generously sharing her wisdom, expertise and fabulous collection of both contemporary and antique whitework. Christine is a talented embroiderer, teacher, collector and author of *Schwalm Embroidery: Techniques and Designs.*

Pieces from Christine's collection appear on pages 7–8, 18–20, 30–31, 56, 60, 73, 77–79, 81–82, 88–89, 118, 122, 144, 147 and 150. The contemporary pieces are all Christine's own work.

A sincere thank you to Lizzie Kulinski also. Lizzie prepared all step-by-step samples and kindly shared her family's whitework heirlooms. These pieces appear on pages 5 and 50.

Thanks also to Yvette Stanton for her Mountmellick pieces on pages 90, 94 and 107.

Finally, thanks to Marjorie Kavanagh, The Last Adieu, *Inspirations* issue 9 featured on page 151, and Berry Millard for Soul Mates.